LOSING HELEN

LOSING HELEN

AN ESSAY

≈

Carol Becker

 Red Hen Press | *Pasadena, CA*

Book layout by Mark E. Cull

Library of Congress Cataloging-in-Publication Data
Names: Becker, Carol, author.
Title: Losing Helen : an essay / Carol Becker.
Description: First Edition. | Pasadena : Red Hen Press, 2016.
Identifiers: LCCN 2016023194 (print) | LCCN 2016024437
(ebook) | ISBN 9781597099905 (pbk. : alk. paper) | ISBN
9781597095099 () Subjects: LCSH: Death—Religious aspects. |
Becker, Helen Hadara, 1909-2005. Classification: LCC BL504
.B43 2016 (print) | LCC BL504 (ebook) | DDC
   818/.603—dc23
LC record available at https://lccn.loc.gov/2016023194

The National Endowment for the Arts, the Los Angeles County
Arts Commission, the Los Angeles Department of Cultural Affairs, the Dwight Stuart Youth Fund, the Pasadena Arts & Culture Commission and the City of Pasadena Cultural Affairs Di-
vision, and Sony Pictures Entertainment partially support Red
Hen Press.

First Edition
Published by Red Hen Press
www.redhen.org

ACKNOWLEDGMENTS

I have always loved the small books writers write after losing a parent: Simone de Beauvoir's *A Very Easy Death,* Philip Roth's *Patriarchy,* Roland Barthes's *Mourning Diary,* Donald Antrim's *The Afterlife,* and the visual/literary essay *Rachel, Monique* by Sophie Calle.

Losing Helen took some time to materialize and to launch in space. I cannot be sure what my mother would have thought about it, but she might have responded like artist Sophie Calle's mother, who, when her daughter put a video camera by the side of her deathbed and set it running, spoke just enough to say: "Finally." Finally I am your subject.

All deaths are equal and yet completely particular to the person, the family, and the situation. The one thing we all share in speaking about the physical loss of a parent is that this inevitability shakes the child self to the core, while it is the adult self who tries to respond in language. All such art making and writing is just an attempt to give this unfathomability form. I am not sure anyone really feels he or she succeeds. Yet, there is an urgency to try.

Losing Helen came from such an impetus, moving me between layers of consciousness and time as I wended my way precariously through Mysticism, Buddhism, and the retirement communities of Florida.

There are many people to acknowledge, living and dead. I mention only those still here, who were there then: Lin Hixson, Litsa Kourti, Matthew Goulish, Lisa Wainwright, Judy Raphael, Susanna Coffey, Roberta Lynch, Kathryn Sapoznick, France Morin, Alda Blanco, Carole Warshaw, Ernesto Pujol, and Jack Murchie.

Thanks to Deborah Cannarella, who brought such wisdom and enthusiasm to the project, to Jean Fulton who has been my editor throughout, and to Kate Gale and Red Hen Press for embracing the text.

I dedicate this small book to the Two Helens.

This essay is about gravity, but, in the spirit of Simone Weil, it is also about grace. I take inspiration from her mystical thinking daily, but in contemplating my mother's death, I defy one of her basic dictums: "All sins are attempts to fill voids."[1] So, inevitably, the following must be full of sin.

LOSING HELEN

I

FIRE: DUST TO DUST

Years before my mother's death, she told me that she already had arranged to be cremated by the Dolphin Club. "They turn your body into ash, then throw you from the back of a boat," she said. At the time, we were setting the table for dinner in her condo in Tamarac, Florida, fanning out the plastic, faux-lace, cream-colored tablecloth we had used for years (even though there were many hand-embroidered linen ones in the breakfront). My knees went weak. I knew I couldn't have this conversation, not then. When I began to cry and told her I simply wasn't ready, she sighed and said lovingly, but with exasperation, "Honey, I'm ninety-three years old. The papers are in the top drawer of your father's dresser." We left it at that.

By most people's standards, my mother was already quite old, but she did not seem old to me. Nor had she ever used that word about herself. She saved "old" for those neighbors fixed in that blank, cloudy, distracted look. Not for her. She still looked glamorous—tall, buxom, *zaftig* really. She walked with pride, wore heels every day, and, most important, had "all her marbles," as in, "Does Helen still have all her marbles?"—a question often asked by my friend Rose, a bit younger than my mother and a Holocaust survivor.

Five years later, my mother, then almost ninety-eight, was in hospice at home. I could no longer avoid the brown envelope and the documents inside. As she had advised, they were amidst the remnants of what had once been my father's dresser. The top drawer still was cluttered with his miscellaneous objects: cuticle scissors; a leather shaving kit for travel; a key ring with an image of a naked woman stretching, forever lodged in a plastic heart; a photo of me that he always carried in his wallet—my twelve-year-old face (bubble hairdo) in a small photo-booth shot—positioned next to some college transcripts. We buried one of these straight-A transcripts with him in his right lapel suit pocket. It was my mother's idea. "He had been so proud," she said, proud that I went to college and had done so well, having himself been kicked out of high school for "shooting craps." My mother, needed by her mother to work the farm, never finished fifth grade. My father had carried those transcripts with him for twenty years, and now for eternity.

We had flown his body north from Florida to be buried in Brooklyn. But when the funeral director opened the coffin and asked me to verify who he was, I said, to everyone's horror, "It's not my father." I was sure. It no longer looked anything like him. The frightened man then called in my mother, who said, "That's George. He's just swollen from weeks on the ventilator. This is the suit I brought to the funeral home, and those are his shoes." It was then that she had the idea to put the transcript in his lapel pocket. But his body was already stiff; I could barely wedge the soft, folded paper inside. We were shattered by his death. How did she have the strength to bring *anything* to the funeral home? Twenty years later, I was still amazed by her composure, and now I was losing her.

The documents were in the drawer, as she said. I noted immediately that her contract was actually with a place called the Neptune Society, but dolphins were close. The contract, for $1,684.62, had been paid in full in small installments, almost ten years before. Clearly my mother didn't want me bothered. Most startling to me was what had been scribbled by her "policy agent" in pen in the corner of the top sheet. It was a note—an addendum, really—"Wants to be buried in the cemetery next to her husband." What happened to the boat and the dolphins?

I called the agency immediately to ask some questions and, in truth, to find out if the Neptune Society really existed. I wanted to know if there were people at the other end of the number on the top of the document at all times. After she died, how would it work? We are not a culture familiar with cremation. What, exactly, do *they* do, and what do *we* do and when?

How long could I keep my mother at home after she died? How much time would it take for someone to come for her? After that, when would she be cremated? When could I get the ashes? It's remarkable to me now that I could even say any of these words to anyone, but, in the thick of it, you do what you have to do.

One month later, my mother was gone. It was early November, and they had told me I'd have to wait a few weeks to claim the ashes. I knew that I would be back in Miami at the beginning of December for the art fair and hoped that I could pick them up then, combined with a visit to her apartment—now *my* apartment—and some time with her friends. I wanted the ashes with me, but I knew I could never pick them up alone, so I had asked my dear friend Lisa to accompany me. She'd also be at Art Basel, and I trusted her to understand what this meant to me but also not to collapse with me. We'd have to go back to Fort Lauderdale to get the box, so we planned the trip for the last day of the fair. I rented a car. Fearful of falling apart, I asked her to drive.

We only had a map and the address. I expected the Neptune Society to be in the older part of Fort Lauderdale, on a cool, tree-lined street. I imagined a discreet place with an unassuming bronze plaque on the side of the door, maybe with just a small trident for the logo. But now I wonder why I ever thought such things. Nothing in Florida is discreet and nothing is old, except the Everglades.

We found the building in a small shopping mall right off Interstate 95. Actually, you couldn't miss it. The huge sign was Neptune himself, embodied as an enormous cutout figure—a barely clad, bearded giant holding an immense plywood trident that towered above the low-rise structures. Here was the god of the sea recast as an anchor-tenant for a depressed mall where half the storefronts were vacant. When we entered the building, however, it was actually quite elegant. It took a moment to discern the dimensions of the room, very somber after the white Florida light. Quiet Muzak surround-sound filled the darkened space. There was a small chapel with velvet chairs to the right of the entrance. To the left, near the reception desk, was a shelf balancing an array of expensive boxes and urns. I had already chosen the simplest metal one, since I knew it would be my mother's preference. "Save your money," she would have said. And it was closest to the Jewish pine coffin.

When they brought out the box, it was larger than I expected. When they handed it to me, it was heavier. Lisa was holding onto my arm. I had to sit down and, of course, immediately began to cry. My beautiful mother—this was all that was left. Nonetheless, I was grateful.

We got into the car, both crying but also laughing—at the place, the rushing traffic, Neptune hovering above us. And there began a new ritual of grief—clutching the metal box, putting it down, picking it up, putting it down, warm tears hitting the cold metal. I did it for months in Chicago—taking the box from my altar, sitting with it in my lap, lighting candles, meditating, then, inevitably, clutching the box again and rocking with it in my arms, crying again, unable to let go. In the hotel room in Miami, I wrapped it in a purple scarf, fearful that it could be stolen—perhaps mistaken for a small jewelry vault. But, really, who would steal such a thing?

The next day I was to leave for Chicago. I knew I could not check the box as luggage. What if it were lost? So, with my carry-on suitcase and the box in a shoulder bag, the letter from the Neptune Society to explain what was in the box in hand, I cautiously approached the security checkpoint. I put the box on the X-ray belt and waited on the other side for it to come through. Of course they stopped me. "What is in this box?" said the guard. "That's my mother," I said, "the remains of my mother. Here are the papers from the funeral home." He turned pale and called others over. Reinforcements? Their faces were bloodless. Had no one ever done this before? "It's very dense," one said. "You should put a coin under it as it goes through, so we can see the coin. Then we'll know it is just dust." Just dust. And a coin for Charon to ferry her across the River Styx.

I got the box home and surrounded it with flowers and candles. I remember hearing that the ashes of my former teacher, Herbert Marcuse, were found in his son's closet decades after his cremation. Someone had misplaced them. How could that be? For me the ashes and bits of bones were so alive, so remarkably heavy and "dense." There would be no forgetting or misplacing them. They now were my mother, all I had. And so I spent several months wrapping and unwrapping that box in various luminous Lao scarves.

Gravity makes things come down, wings make them rise.[2]

Over many years of travel, I had evolved a very elaborate altar in my Chicago house. It had begun quite unselfconsciously with a small Burmese wooden Buddha, a gift from friends Lin and Matthew, installed with some candles and flowers on a low table I had bought at a rummage sale for just that purpose. But soon the objects grew and migrated—first to the mantelpiece, then down the sides and to the base of the fireplace, and, finally, onto another small desk across the room, until the altar became the predominant fixture of the combined living/dining room.

The altar—now a large, chaotic installation—comprises small objects, miniscule in some cases: roughly carved wooden animals from Zimbabwe; bronze miniature tourist "Emerald Buddhas" from Thailand; soft, black-clad warrior dolls from Chiapas holding miniature cloth rifles, their faces masked; a highly polished wooden Buddha from Korea; a transparent blue polyurethane one from Laos; sepia-toned photos of my mother and father—each captured when they were young and beautiful; an old photo of me and my too-early-departed friend, Kathy Acker; a section devoted to all things Mayan, with a flat stone carving of a diving Goddess Ix Chel and small, cross-legged ceramic Mayan statuettes (some in fragments), to whom I pay homage each Friday when they are thought to be on Earth doing good deeds. For all this and more, I light candles, sometimes flooding the whole altar with light or just sparsely illuminating one section at a time. During the period when I still had the ashes, they were its axis.

It wasn't until some months later, when I was in Rome, that I had a revelation. I had come to the American Academy to write. I knew I could not bring the ashes. But in the sparseness of my room, my dreams were vivid and my sadness uninterrupted. One night I had an auditory dream, or that's how I have come to think of them—dreams without image but with language. When these occur, there is usually a phrase or sentence that is spoken to me while I am asleep. The meaning of the sentence is usually immediately clear, although the words are never as I would have constructed them when awake. This particular night, I heard my mother say, "Put the ashes to rest." In this dream state, she and I negotiated when this should occur. My mother wanted me to bury them as soon as I returned. I wanted to wait until it was warmer—preferably summer—when it would not feel so cold and I would not feel so desolate. Not when it was dark and bitter, I insisted. I just couldn't.

We went back and forth about the date, but I must have won, because after I returned to Chicago in March, I picked a day in July when I would return to New York with the ashes for the burial.

Sometime later, I came across a story about a woman named Rani, a great devotee of the Goddess Kali. Rani married a man of extreme wealth and, after he died, she took hold of his business, accruing even more riches. Knowing little about finances, she attributed all her success to Kali—the gracious mother of the universe, but also the fierce figure hung with the arms and heads of corpses who helps us all to reconcile death and destruction.

Rani vowed to build a temple to Kali. For its centerpiece, she commissioned a renowned artist to sculpt a very large image of the goddess. He created a magnificent piece out of black basalt for Kali and white marble for Shiva. But Rani procrastinated and did not fix a date for the dedication of her temple. So, although the statue was finished, it remained packed in a crate, waiting. One night Rani had a dream, and Kali spoke to her: "How long will you keep me confined in this way? I feel suffocated." Needless to say, Rani quickly chose a date to inaugurate the temple. When the workers finally unhinged the crate to remove the image of the goddess, they were astonished to find the statue wet with perspiration.[3]

Negotiating the *Landsmanshaftn*[4]

~

In my search for the cremation documents, I found my mother's records of her contributions to the Citron Circle. Each year she paid twelve dollars for herself and twelve dollars for me for the upkeep of our burial plots in the family circle—the *Landsmanshaftn*. In Poland and Russia, Jews had established organizations designed to keep families together in life. But one of their functions also was to serve as burial societies, a very nineteenth-century notion that was carried over to the "new world." Families buried together stayed together—forever.

The Citron Circle is the family organization of my father's mother—my grandmother Esther, née Esther Citron. All of her family, who had come to the States from Russia, including my great-grandparents, is buried there, as well as all the Beckers (my father's family). Everyone from the Jewish side whom I had loved as a child is there—my grandmother, aunts, uncles, great-aunts, great-uncles, and even cousins of my generation who died young. Becker is not German but, rather, a phonetic interpretation of the Russian name my grandfather spoke to the authorities when he landed at Ellis Island. Whatever they heard, Becker is what they wrote down.

The New Jersey cemetery site was farmland when the Citron Circle bought this large plot so far from Brooklyn where they all lived. There probably was no land left to buy in more conveniently located cemeteries by the time the family arrived. They knew they needed a good-sized parcel to anticipate all the generations to come. Still, New Jersey must have seemed like the Wild West.

The cemetery is a Spartan place. Once Jews left the Russian *shtetls*, where cemeteries were ancient and chaotic, they constructed very orderly cemeteries—austere, actually, with only small, uniform shrubbery allowed. The Citron Circle is a rather lovely setting at the edge of the cemetery. There used to be a few low shrubs planted next to each grave, as I had done for my mother. Since then, the Circle decided the maintenance was too costly, so they ripped most of them out, including hers. But my father still has his shrub. He also has a special brass stake in the ground that indicates he was a World War II veteran. Perhaps no one had the heart to remove all of that history.

As often as I'd visited, I had never before dealt with the business office of the cemetery. I had no idea what would be involved. I knew that the first step would be to find out if they allowed those who had been cremated to be buried in the cemetery. So I called, befriending the first person I talked to, trying to make an alliance—knowing, intuitively, that this would not be simple. I asked the first question and held my breath: Could someone who had been cremated be buried in the cemetery? Yes, it could be done. There had been some cremated bodies buried there. Yes, they knew the Citron Circle. But, before they could agree to a burial, I had to get permission from the woman in charge (a cousin I did not know) who represented the Circle. They needed her to tell them which plot was my mother's.

They gave me her number, and I called and spoke to a great-cousin whom I had never met. Her father was my grandmother's brother, Max. I actually remembered Max, a handsome man who suffered from varicose veins and gout, as all my grandmother's brothers had. It was his daughter who was in charge. When I called, she told me that, yes, my mother had a plot, but the plot was not *next* to my father's as my mother had specified, because his brothers—Max and Hymie—were there. Rather, it was to the east of my father, behind his stone. They would be head-to-head or toe-to-toe. Then I told her that the body had been cremated and that the cemetery had approved the burial. I wanted her to know. She was surprised that it was acceptable for Jews to be cremated, but did not challenge it. "We all loved your mother," she said. "She was very beautiful. But your mother was not Jewish, as I remember. Did she convert?" I took a breath. "No, my mother was not Jewish. But I am Jewish," I said (although this is not technically true—by Orthodox Jewish law, since my mother was not Jewish, neither am I). Silence on the other end. "There will be a rabbi," I quickly added. "He will preside." I held my breath again. Deep pause now. "Well, as long as there is a rabbi. . . ." I breathed out. Now I needed to find a rabbi.

Twenty years ago, for my father's "unveiling," my cousin Ellie had arranged for the rabbi. To our amazement, he arrived quite late, driving a small, red sports car with a license plate that read, "My Toy." Not him, I thought. I won't call him. I needed a serious rabbi in whom I could confide and who would be okay with all of this. I called Beulah, the mother of my dear friend Carole. She knew such things, was a wonderful person to talk to, and lived in New Jersey. Her family was also buried in Beth-El. I knew she would help. She gave me the name of a retired rabbi who lived in her building. He was her friend, and they both lived close to the cemetery.

I called. "Of course I'll help," he said. We talked for some time. I told him about my mother. I told him she was not Jewish. He did not care. I told him about the cremation. He did not care. I asked him how much he would charge. He did not want money. "I will not charge for this, but you can donate something to my synagogue, if you'd like. Whatever amount you choose is fine." He was kind, and I was relieved. We picked a Friday in early July. "A blessing to be buried so close to the Sabbath," the rabbi observed. I would have to fly from Chicago. I hoped it would not rain and that a few people would come. I prepared myself to turn over the ashes. I had a little time. I lit candles. I spoke to her photos. I said we were on our way. I hoped she was pleased.

July came too fast, and once again I was at the airport carrying the metal box. Because I now knew this could cause a problem, I told the security woman on the far side of the X-ray machine what was in the box. And before I put it on the belt, I offered the letter from the Neptune Society as verification of the contents. I gave her a minute to digest what I had said. She looked blank then yelled across the checkpoint, "Hey, this woman here has her mother's ashes and wants to put them through the X-ray. Have you done that before?" Several guards immediately rushed over. All of them now were looking at the box, picking it up and turning it over. And by then, of course, all the passengers waiting in line were looking at me sorrowfully. "Hey, Miss, it's okay, put the box on the belt." Then one by one the security guards came toward me and, as if rehearsed, said in succession, "Sorry for your loss."

II

EARTH: BURIAL

In order to be sure we would get to the cemetery on time, we—my then partner, now husband, Jack, and I—came from Chicago the night before and slept in my small Brooklyn apartment. Of course I woke up early, agitated. I could hear the rain. It was torrential, what I had most dreaded. But at least it wasn't cold. We left for New Jersey with plenty of time to get there. I was worried that we would be ensnarled in traffic and that we simply might not be able to find the cemetery. It had been so long.

My father, who ran the auction room on the boardwalk at Point Pleasant, New Jersey for many years, always got lost getting to New Jersey. If they changed a sign or moved a lamppost, he'd get lost, and he'd always say, as if for the first time, "Where the hell's New Jersey?" Can someone lose a state? He and I, alone or together—not my mother, who always knew where she was—could lose a state. Jack, like my mother, always finds his way—he has a built-in compass, while I am missing the chip. Nonetheless, it was not a day to gamble. The weather was "rotten," as my mother might have said. Some of her nieces and nephews were meeting us there, as were Beulah and the rabbi. We gave ourselves lots of time.

This was a good thing because we had to pull over several times. Water flooded the sewers and then the streets. We were unable to see out the windows. My mother had died in the wake of a hurricane. Now she would be buried in a downpour. What else could we have expected? There were stories of great Buddhas whose death had caused the earth to shatter with thunder. I didn't think my mother was a Bodhisattva, but she was powerful in her way, always the one to rescue people in need, to know the right thing to do, unflappable. Water is always connected to the Goddess Kali. In fact, after rituals for Ma Kali are complete, the actual worship is directed to "the pot-like vessel" filled with water, which represents the Great Mother herself—"the cosmic womb."[5]

I had been instructed that when we arrived at the cemetery, we first must check in at the office. When we finally did arrive at the gates, this is what we did. Jack parked the car. I went in first, holding the box, now wrapped in a blue Vietnamese silk scarf. I signed in at the desk, wrote what seemed to be an exorbitant check for the burial, and so we began.

"Is that the box?" asked the woman behind the counter. "I'll come around." She grabbed the box out of my arms, the scarf dropped to the floor. She then started turning it upside down as if she were looking for an opening or as if it were a puzzle she was trying to figure out. "Where are the papers for this?" she asked brusquely. "What papers?" I said. "The ones that say who is in the box." "Who is in the box?" I repeated, astonished. "Are you kidding? Who would be in this box? It's my mother, of course." "How do I know that?" she said. "I called one hundred times, over the past months," I said. "I've talked to everyone who works here. No one ever mentioned that I had to bring papers. I have papers, but I left them in Brooklyn. I only brought them for airport security. It never occurred to me that you'd ask. Who else could this be? Do you think this is some mob hit that I'm fronting? Who else would I bury in my mother's plot in the Citron Circle next to my father except my mother? Who?" I was yelling and crying now. "I don't know who," said the woman, "but this box is not getting buried until I know who is in it. There will be no burial without papers." I collapsed in a chair. At this point, Jack, with atypical anger, got between the woman and me, shouting at her, "Do you think this is a hardware store, and she's trying to return a tool and you get to say, 'No, we won't take it back?' This is her mother who has a plot here. This has been planned for months. We came from Chicago. There's a rabbi. There's family. There is no coming back next week. She has to bury her mother now."

At this point we were making so much noise that another woman came around to the front. She was trying to be calm. "Can you explain the problem?" "Yes, we can," I said. "Dear, where did your mother get cremated? Do you know?" "Yes, I know. Of course I know—the Neptune Society in Fort Lauderdale." "Let's call them," she said calmly. "They can fax over the paper that is needed. No one has to scream. Come back to the office with me."

I sat in a chair, head in hands, sobbing, and then found the number. Luckily it was Friday and not a weekend, and a human was there to pick up the phone. They soon faxed over the necessary papers, and we were on our way. But the box, where

21

was the box? I found it shoved into a corner on someone's desk. The ashes I had cherished for months, cried over for months, now were someone's paperweight. My mother and I were just trying to get her buried. Why was this so hard?

"Okay, dear. We are all set," the kind woman said. "Wait here. You can follow the truck to the cemetery. They will come with you to bury your mother. Don't cry."

Jack went to get our car. I was worried about the rabbi, the small family group we had assembled, all waiting at the plot. It had gotten so late. I called Beulah to say we were almost there.

Jack pulled the rental car up behind the pickup truck that we had been instructed to follow. One man got out. He took the box from me. "Follow us," he said. The other man waited in the truck. There were shovels in the boot. The men were dressed like gardeners about to dig up some weeds. Pretty funky, but we followed.

When we got to the site, I let Jack deal with the burial crew. I rushed over to the rabbi, Beulah, and the small group of cousins to explain what had just happened. The rabbi was infuriated. "This is how they treat people at the hardest moments of their life? This is a great embarrassment. I've talked to them about such behavior before. All they care about is the money, and they charge too much."

Jack called me over. "The gardeners want to know where to begin to dig." I was confused that there was not already a hole. I had always thought it would be a big hole, as it would be for a coffin. Only then did I realize that of course it would be a small but deep hole. (And for this I had just paid hundreds of dollars?) "Here, dig here," I said, having walked around the plot to decide.

It's hard to fathom what happened next, and luckily I was too busy conferring with the rabbi to see this myself, but Jack recounted it to me later. Apparently, the driver of the pickup told the other man, "Get the box from the truck." Perhaps the second man did not speak English very well because he returned shortly carrying a family-size, very empty plastic Pepsi bottle that he had taken from the front seat of the truck. He was holding it out in front of him, moving extremely carefully, as if it were something very precious. Then, as in a Laurel and Hardy routine, the driver said to the other man, "Not the Pepsi bottle, stupid, the ashes. Get the box with the ashes." Had it actually been a Laurel and Hardy movie and had the two men been closer, Hardy surely would have whacked Laurel upside the head.

If it weren't my mother, if it weren't her burial, if it weren't all so wrenching, this surely would have made me laugh.

When the rabbi and I first moved away to talk, he said, "Tell me about your mother and tell me about her death." I told him how she had come to New York from a small mining town in Pennsylvania when she was fifteen years old, how her father had died in the mines, and her mother had raised ten children. Life had not been easy, but she had had a very close family. My mother was strong. Her mother was the same. They were powerful women, resourceful. My mother was resilient, grateful, interested in the world and in people. While our life together had not been without tension, and there had always been a barrier between us that I could not understand, I adored her. When I told the rabbi that she was almost ninety-eight years old when she died and that her last months were spent at her home with me, in hospice care, he said, "She helped you come into the world, and you helped her leave. It doesn't get more perfect than that."

The Stones

~

The presence of the dead person is imaginary, but his absence is very real; henceforward it is his way of appearing.[6]

Jews don't bring flowers to graves. They bring stones. But no one is certain exactly why. There are many theories. People used to be buried under piles of stones. Stones were used to secure tombs to keep the dead, dead, and not walking the planet as ghosts. But I like best the thought that stones, like souls, endure. I always placed stones on the graves of my uncles, aunts, and grandparents. The stones I brought this time were small. I'd been collecting them on my travels for months. But soon I ran short and thought about whom I had loved most, whom I had really wanted to tell that I'd been here. All the big personalities of my childhood, all my great loves from the Jewish side of my family were in this graveyard. There could never be enough stones. At other sites, I noticed that people had left large stones—boulders, even—for their loved ones. I just had small, little jewels—petrified wood from the island of Mytilene, Petoskey stones from the shores of Lake Michigan, and quartz from the jungles of Belize.

It was odd that my mother couldn't be next to my father after so many years of marriage. But he was beside his two brothers, one of whom he had loved and with whom he had worked closely in business—my Uncle Hymie, who had died at fifty years old when I was ten. His other brother, Max, he never really admired. My mother would be behind them all.

At the foot of her plot was my cousin Eleanor, who also had died too young and who had converted to Catholicism to please her Italian husband and children. She must have asked to be buried here with her parents in spite of this conversion and in spite of its meaning—being separated from her husband and family for eternity. But it was always hard to imagine Eleanor Catholic. When it came down to it, and I guess death is as "down to it" as it gets, she wanted to be with all of us. I don't blame her. She'd have understood the caper my mother and I had just pulled off. She knew about mixed marriages and being ostracized. She got pregnant before marriage, and shame hung over her for her whole life. Her "situation" shadowed all the girls of our family who came after. No one seemed to recover. "Don't be like Ellie," they'd tell us. "She ruined her life." But did she? It never seemed like that to me. Why had they abandoned her? She loved her husband and her family. She was devoted to her parents. But it was the 1950s, and the man with whom she got pregnant was Italian, from the rougher part of the neighborhood. "What good could come of that?" they all thought. And yet much good had.

Next to my mother was an unoccupied plot. That, of course, was for me.

The fear of illegitimacy—or should I say shame?—was not new to us. In truth, my mother and I were both impersonating Jews our whole lives. My mother had never renounced Catholicism. Rather, she had just let it slide. She didn't mind being the only non-Jew in her Jewish world. After my father died, she even joined *Hadassah* and helped serve Saturday bagels and lox at the clubhouse. Right after his death, when the neighbors asked if we were going to "sit *shivah*"—the seven-day mourning ritual of renunciation for the immediate family right after a death—she said, "No, we are not Orthodox." When they left, I said to her, "'Not Orthodox,' Mom? We're not even Jewish."

There was always this difference between us and the rest of our Jewish world. But, on this day, none of it mattered. The rabbi didn't care. The family circle didn't care. In the end, the cemetery didn't care. She had been loved, she got to be where she had chosen, and I had helped. And yet, there was the fear, up until the last moment, that it would all be taken away—this right to fit in, even at the grave, because we only partially ever did.

Shame

〜

I was the product of an unorthodox union, radical for its time. I was therefore a blessing—special, out of the ordinary. But I was also a hybrid, a mix, a *mishling*. In this union there was shame. Why else would my parents have hidden their marriage from both their families for a year and then only told them because they had to?

My father's friend Charlie, a.k.a. Blubber, a former prize-fighter with big boxer lips, had been using my parents' apartment during the day to "run a numbers operation." My mother did not know. My father had told him he could use the apartment when they were at work. But, when she came home one evening from her job making wigs and giving scalp treatments at Evanthes in Times Square, the house was surrounded by police. She did not go in. After the bust, my parents were forced to move. This is all I know about it. But somewhere in this mayhem, my mother felt she had to tell her mother that she was not living alone anymore and that she and "Georgie" had gotten married. My father, often called Gorgeous George, was a charismatic guy. He also was a gambler when my mother met him. This worried my mother, but he was irresistibly confident, naturally funny, and good to the core. How could my mother resist? But it did take her ten years to agree to marry him. What my Catholic mother feared most was the ostracism of his Jewish family.

My Aunt Harriet, my father's sister, could not abide that my parents were hiding their marriage. She insisted that she take my mother to meet her mother—my Jewish grandmother, Esther. She knew that my grandmother was an extraordinary person—very gentle and very warm. She was married to a narcissistic man she never really loved, an arranged marriage that took place once they came to America from Russia. What follows is the story of the day my mother met my grandmother, as told to me by both my mother and my aunt.

My Jewish grandparents lived in Brooklyn, close to Crown Heights. My mother (how nervous she must have been) went with my Aunt Harriet to meet my grandmother. My mother—tall, beautiful, with sandy-colored hair swept up—was always dressed like a movie star. This day she was all in white, with a large-brimmed hat. Harriet, my favorite of my father's sisters, was very dark skinned. She had been an embarrassment to my father, her older brother, who was teased whenever he took her out in the carriage, because she "looked black" to his boyhood friends. So embarrassed was he by all of this that he had once "traded her for a puppy." He thought he'd gotten a good deal—racism ran deep—until he had to explain to my grandmother where her daughter was. Frantic, my grandmother hit the streets and found her. In spite of this, my father and my aunt became great friends.

That auspicious day when my aunt took my mother home to her mother, my grandmother knew who she was the minute she opened the door. "You are Georgie's wife," she said, embracing my mother. She then took off her wedding ring and gave it to my mother to wear. After that day, they were always close. My mother learned to cook my grandmother's recipes. They confided in each other. Much later, when my grandmother had a stroke and couldn't speak, she chose to come and recuperate with us. Although two of her daughters had married successful businessmen and lived in large houses with servants in Flatbush, she wanted to stay in our three-room apartment in Crown Heights and sleep in our only bedroom, while we all slept in the living room—my parents on the convertible. It was where she felt most at home. I loved that time with my grandmother. I can see her clearly still in her pink, satin, quilted bed jacket, as I flashed small image cards in front of her to get her to say the words.

My grandfather, who had wanted to become a rabbi, locked himself in his room on that important day, refusing to come out. But, over time, and after my grandmother and my Uncle Hymie (with whom he lived) both died, he also came to live with us. By then we had a large house in East Flatbush. My mother kept a kosher kitchen for him, something my father never understood. "Why do you bother? He won't know the difference," my father would say. "Because I promised," she'd respond. "I will not betray him." In spite of this apparent acceptance, there was shame. And it existed on the other side as well. The Polish Catholics taunted me as a child; they were certain my mother and I would burn in Hell.

So we were neither Catholic nor Jewish. We had entered the tribe, but we were not of the tribe. Yet my mother had paved the way. Later, when my cousin Eli brought home a Catholic girl whom he wanted to marry, it was easier for everyone to accept her. They said, "We love Helen. We could love this woman, too." And they did.

I was drawn to Judaism. I asked to study Hebrew when I was young, and since all the boys in the family had no interest, my grandfather was stuck with me. I learned the *Haggadah* for Passover. I asked the Four Questions. I recited the

Kaddish. I went to synagogue with my grandfather, and, after my grandmother died, only he and I cared about getting the rituals right. Yet I still was not pure. I was a mix. The ancient Greeks had the concept of "pollution," which had the power to spill out and over from the original situation onto all that surrounded it. Pollution could contaminate and create miasma. These were external conditions. Internally, there was shame, and, as Sandra Edelman explains in *Turning the Gorgon*, it was "indeterminate, complex . . . polysemic, never in a state of equilibrium," able to attach to all things.[7]

The Jungians talk about wounded narcissism—an early condition, an open sore that one carries through the world. It is a neurotic effect that is constantly trying to protect us. Yet one expects to be jostled; the wound is always ready to be reopened if one is not vigilant. "Anticipatory fear," Edelman calls it, the fear of being wounded again.[8] Shame exists even in the shame of feeling ashamed.[9] There are many things that might cause this, but the result is always the same—to feel defective in relationship to an ideal or a purity that, for whatever reason, cannot be upheld.

My mother seemed unaffected by all this. She was a very proud woman and practical. She had been on her own in New York since she was quite young. She was not insecure in herself. But there were situations, and the religion conundrum was one of them, that she simply did not want to confront. This is why she waited so long to marry my father even though he adored her. She did not want to be the *goyim*.

Having launched us all into this complexity, my parents really had no idea how it affected me. They told me I would someday have to choose: Jewish or Catholic. They could not have imagined that this would become my greatest source of anxiety. In this originary drama, how could I really ever choose? If I declared myself Catholic, I would be ostracized by the Jewish family. And I never could really say I was Jewish since my mother had not converted, and, anyway, I then would have chosen against the Catholic family. So I was hovering, exploring always, but anxious that I would make the wrong choice. To this day, when I get caught, unable to choose between this or that (always small matters, never large ones), I am reminded of the Jewish-Catholic dilemma for which there never was a right resolution. At such moments, I might just as well flip a coin.

Somehow my parents never understood what the world had done to them, how it had made them insecure, worried about getting married at all, about telling their families. And as generous as they both were in so many ways, they never extrapolated from their situation to a greater generosity around race. I paid dearly for this blind spot when my father disowned me several decades ago for having a relationship with a man of mixed race. They couldn't see why I would be drawn to someone with such social complexity. What had he to do with me? And so the drama continued, and the stigma now fell on my choices and the shame I was bringing to them.

Florida I

~

When my parents were seventy-six years old, they decided to move from Brooklyn to Tamarac in Broward County, Florida, not far from Fort Lauderdale. This was a huge surprise. Unlike my aunts and uncles, they were not people who went to Florida in the winters. But my father had been very ill; the prognosis was not good. The cold had become very difficult for him. My mother wanted to move someplace warm where he could at least get out and walk. So, unbeknownst to me, they sold the house in East Flatbush and announced that they were moving to Florida.

It was a great rupture for them to leave Brooklyn—so traumatic that it was never discussed. My mother had sold the house right out from under my father. She had made the decision—he couldn't handle the winters anymore. And she couldn't watch him trapped, caged in his vulnerability. By selling the Brooklyn house, they could buy something in Florida. With my aunt and uncle already at the Bermuda Club, a large apartment complex, my mother believed it could work. To move at seventy-six was brave, perhaps reckless, I feared. For my mother, it was essential. She always had good instincts about life—what she needed and when—and she was confident she could make it work.

At the time of this relocation, my father was still able to get around. He'd go to the delicatessen in the morning in Tamarac, sit at the counter, read the paper, have a bagel—not unlike his life in Brooklyn. On his way home, he'd invariably bump into an overly friendly neighbor, usually a widowed woman. When he'd return to the apartment, he'd say, "What's with these people? They tell you to 'have a nice day.' What the hell is it to them?"

Florida was a world he did not understand—small shopping malls everywhere filled with transient businesses. And if you wanted to pay cash for a car instead of buying on credit, they'd charge you more. "The crooks," my father said. "What kind of place is this?"

When they first moved to Tamarac there were still parts of the landscape that were wild and jungle-like. Everything had a damp feel. The closets got moldy. Nothing dried. From time to time there were enormously fat toads in the elevators. The displaced New York neighbors were scared of these creatures and some called the police—to alert them, as if they'd seen aliens. "What do you want us to do?" said the police. But my mother had grown up on a farm. She loved the white herons, storks, and ducks resting in the human-made canals that caught the currents from the Everglades. She was grateful that she lived on the water, that there was light. Even the fake ponds and faux bridges connecting the three-story buildings of her complex made her proud.

They did their best to adjust. In the first years they took trips up and down the coast. They made friends. Having been on cruises, they knew how to fit in. They went to "shows" at the clubhouse and they once had been one of three couples called up out of the audience to the stage. They were the best looking and the most "with it," by far. They won the prize because they both remembered that "their song" was Fats Domino singing, "I found my thrill, on Blueberry Hill. On Blueberry Hill, when I found you."

Soon my father became too familiar with the local doctors. My trips down south became about visiting him in various emergency rooms in Tamarac—beige, overly air-conditioned, metallic. Once stabilized, he'd often escape from these hospitals, calling from some phone booth on a nondescript corner, wanting to be "picked up." I often had trouble finding him. We were always lost in Tamarac, new to suburban streets that all looked the same, and my parents didn't believe in maps.

At first my father talked about opening another business, a small "outlet store." But soon his partner-to-be had a heart attack and died. And my father also was fading; some years before he had had blood clots in his lungs. Cigarettes, years of them, had turned his lungs to tissue paper. His circulation was "bad," his color "not good," although he still was a handsome man, something like the actor Ben Gazzara. (I remember this each day because I carry his Florida driver's license in my wallet, next to my own.)

But on my first visit, it was different. My father was feeling "himself." He even picked me up at the Fort Lauderdale airport as he had always done at LaGuardia. But this time he was wearing white pants, shiny, patent-leather, beige shoes with gold-plated buckles, and a beige shirt. His car was cream with a tan interior. When I commented on this new suburban, monochromatic look, he responded, "When in Rome . . ."

I carry my father's driver's license in my wallet because it was not easy for him to get. He had always had a car. But he had to take the Florida driving exam when they moved. After failing the first time, he was determined to pass. And, finally, he did. Once it was clear that my father was getting worse and that my mother probably would be on her own sometime soon, my mother knew she needed to learn to drive—something that had never been necessary in Brooklyn. She looked in the Yellow Pages and found a driving school. The young Puerto Rican woman who taught her became her close friend. She wrote to me after my mother died to say that my mother had been by far her oldest pupil and her most beloved.

The Bermuda Club

~

Like so many places in Florida called the Shores, the Riviera, the Palms, or the Flamingo, the Bermuda Club is a complex of stand-alone buildings with about twenty-five apartments in each and thirty or so buildings in all. Every cluster of buildings has a small pool, and there is one large "clubhouse" surrounded by tennis and bocce ball courts, a cabana area, and a larger pool. This is where the events take place—the *Hadassah* meetings, "the shows"—comedians, singers, and actors brought in from the Borscht Belt circuit to entertain the condo owners.

Initially my parents rented an apartment "to see if they liked it." But my father was very aware that he was failing quickly and he soon insisted that they buy a unit. He wanted my mother to be secure. They paid $23,000 for a two-bedroom condo with chartreuse shag carpet throughout; darker-green-and-silver, swirling, shiny, raised wallpaper in the dining room; and a completely pink guest toilet. In the twenty years my mother lived in that apartment, she never changed a thing.

Some people, like my parents, lived in the apartments all year round. Others, the "snow birds," came only for the winter. No matter their status, the compass point for the Bermuda Club was always oriented to true north—New York and, sometimes, New Jersey.

As the inhabitants were all northern transplants, they brought with them the delicatessens, bakeries, and ways of life from New York (originally from Eastern Europe). The Bermuda Club was mostly Jewish, and, like many of the other developments in Tamarac, there were also always some Italians in the mix. But the jokes, the *shticks*, were always Jewish.

When my parents first arrived, the Bermuda Club was flourishing. People sat around the pools during the winter months reading the paper, commenting on phone calls they'd gotten from up north where there was ice, slush, snow, and freezing rain. They loved thinking of all the weather nightmares they were missing. They, who had worked so hard every day of their lives, who rode the subway and suffered the stifling heat and dense cold of New York for thirty years, had come to Florida for two weeks in the winter and had dreamt of a life there. My parents were not like this. It will always amaze me that they left their friends, family, and beloved Italian neighbors—the Napolis—to move to Florida.

But I enjoyed the Bermuda Club and thought of writing a sitcom about it—people coming in and out, replicating the life of Brooklyn apartment buildings. It was casual and familiar. It was like *The Golden Girls*, or some Jewish version of the show. My parents seemed happy. I met their friends. The stories of their new neighbors were terrific. There was always something extreme happening up north that needed the attention of the entire building down south. A distraught neighbor with grown kids would come into our apartment with a deep concern: "My son has joined a cult. What should I do?" My mother always offered advice.

In the years after I left Brooklyn for California and then Chicago, they lived in a big house in East Flatbush next to what was then the BMT subway, now the D train—the Newkirk Avenue stop. I never spent much time there—only the last years of high school, then summers and holidays when I returned from college and later graduate school. While in Tamarac we were again compressed into a small apartment, but this one was significantly bigger and better than the three rooms we shared in Crown Heights. It had a guest/TV room where I could sleep. The building had a pool. It was bright. And I soon discovered where to find the *New York Times*.

But right when they arrived, my Uncle Joe died. My Aunt Harriet, suddenly alone, sunk into sadness. Over the next twenty years, the neighbors grew old, became ill, and expired.

Among the early losses was Beatrice's husband. Beatrice and Dave lived next door to my parents. Dave had Alzheimer's, but in the early stages the doctors said it was just "memory loss and disorientation." He often couldn't find his way home. Florence's husband was also ill and died soon after. Her husband would run his car into the hedges bordering the parking lot. About these incidents, it was said, "He forgot he was driving." And "Paul next door"—"Pablo," as my mother liked to call him—also was ailing. He collapsed onto his kitchen floor one day. His wife, Harriet, came running in to get my mother to help pick him up. They knew she was still strong.

The men were falling apart. There were jokes about it—bawdy, cruel jokes that made them laugh. Here's one: A woman complains to her friend that there is something seriously wrong with her husband, and the doctors say it could be Alzheimer's or AIDS. The friend thinks for a moment and then says, "Okay, this is what you do: Take him out in the woods and leave him there. If he finds his way home, don't fuck him."

It wasn't long before my father was suffering. He would sit up all night in the "Bermuda Room," watching television or dozing, terrified to lie down, his lungs so brittle they easily would fill with water, unable to contract sufficiently to pump it out—pulmonary edema, they called it. He felt as if he were suffocating or drowning. The Bermuda Room was a screened-in porch overlooking the faux canals, separated from the rest of the house by sliding glass doors and the cacophony of birds and frogs.

In the entrance to the apartment was a very small, hexagonal, green-and-yellow Tiffany-style glass shade hanging from a brass chain. They had brought it with them from Brooklyn, probably from one of my auctioneer father's stores, or "stocks," as he always called them. It once had hung in the foyer of their East Flatbush home. When my mother called the paramedics for my father—which was becoming a weekly event—one of those who came often was a tall guy, even taller than my father, named Walter, whom they liked. When Walter rushed into the apartment to help, he always hit his head on the glass fixture. One day my father said, "Let's get the chain shortened, so Walter won't hit his head." He knew the visits were not going to end.

Trips to the Bermuda Club became increasingly sad. I could never spend more than a few days. If I did, I would become weighted down with the illness and creeping decay around me. I felt continuously connected to death, like those monks who sleep in their coffins each night. There were times when I couldn't breathe in the apartment—or outside, for that matter. It was a subdued anxiety, the anxiety of impending loss. Then I'd walk. Along the way would be Bermuda Clubbers doing laps around the complex wearing clean, white running shoes their kids probably sent from up north to keep them walking and prevent them from shrinking further, getting osteoporosis, or succumbing to heart attacks.

Over time their world narrowed even more. Friends died. My father died—slowly, painfully, after open-heart surgery. My Aunt Harriet died. My mother, constantly inventive, made new friends, but they, too, died. It was as if the air in the place was leaking out slowly, and the space was sucking itself in.

I always felt choked by the humidity, the sidewalks stained with green algae, jackfruit, and other pungent tropical pods crushed underfoot. I'd walk to the Publix market to get a *New York Times*, desperate for a sense that somewhere, life as I remembered it was still being lived.

Twenty years later, my mother often stood outside the apartment, leaning on the third-floor railing, looking down at the parking lot. "The place has changed," she'd say. "There's no life here anymore. Everyone is old." And she was right. I am not sure what she saw then. Perhaps that no one seemed to take their cars out of their parking spaces anymore or that so many of the neighbors were gone. But when she said this, I sensed that she, too, was preparing to leave. The place now depressed her. This scared me, and I'd turn away, unwilling to see how vulnerable she, too, had become.

Florida II

Don't get me wrong. There had been many wonderful trips to Florida—first, to see my parents and, later, after my father died, twenty more years of visiting my mother and Aunt Helen—her beloved sister-in-law who lived with her for part of the year after her husband, my mother's brother Jakie, died. Many birthdays, Mother's Days, Thanksgivings, Christmases, many trips en route to Belize, when landing in Fort Lauderdale provided a welcome chance to see my family, to swim in the ocean, and escape the Chicago cold. But toward the end, her end, landing in Fort Lauderdale was always accompanied by a sense of deep dread. This dread had begun with my father's prolonged suffering.

I had run down so many times expecting his death. There was once a call from my mother to the School of the Art Institute where I taught. Because she had never called me at work, I knew he was bad. Although that was not the time, it was becoming clear that the end was close. Still, I was not prepared. When it finally did come, I arrived in the morning, too late. He had died alone the night before. They had called my mother at midnight to say it was probably going to happen in the next hours, but my mother had asked not to be called until the morning (afraid to hear this news while alone). By the time I arrived, plans were already under way. My mother and her closest friend at that time were taking his suit and shoes to the funeral home. We didn't see him again until we met the coffin at the funeral home in Brooklyn.

But with my mother, it was different. I was determined that she would not be alone. We were preparing for her death together, although we never spoke a word about it.

In the last years, she had become more and more housebound. If it wasn't that she felt tired, it was that her "equilibrium was off," and she was dizzy. Before I arrived, we would make plans to go shopping or to the movies. Then she'd cancel when I got there. She just didn't feel well enough. She now seldom went out. Everything and everyone came to her, even the woman who cut her hair. Her world was constricting. And, most significant, I knew she was bored.

One day she fell by the refrigerator and could not get up. She had not pressed the button on the electronic device she had been wearing around her neck for years (at my insistence). That device, designed for just such events, would have connected her to a service. First they would have alerted me, then her neighbors, then 911. Instead, she waited for hours until Beatrice, the woman from Colombia who helped her through the last months, arrived. When I asked why she had not pressed the button, she said she thought it was pressed "only" if she had a "heart attack." Of course, pride was the real reason. She probably thought she could get up by herself. But she could not.

When she slid off the couch some months later, unable to pull herself back up, Beatrice called me in Chicago. I was driving, on my way to a dinner at the home of the South African Consul General, who was living in the elegant Chicago suburb of Winnetka. Even before I heard about the fall, I had been planning to take a plane to Fort Lauderdale the next morning. But now it was too late to get there that evening, and my mother had told them absolutely not to call 911. I asked to speak to her. She said she was fine and that she could get up if she wanted to, but she did not want to. I knew that she probably could not get up on her own and simply could not say this. Not wanting to humiliate her further, I asked if she'd like to just sleep there on the rug. I told Beatrice to make her comfortable for the night. This was behavior that I'd not witnessed before.

The dinner at the Consul General's was a superb gourmet meal, but I could not eat. I could not make conversation. I called Beatrice several times in tears. I could only think of my mother sleeping on that green shag rug, and that this was probably the end, slowly closing in.

The Dream

~

My Polish grandmother and my mother were both psychic. I grew up with séances and with tea-leaf, coffee-ground, and palm readings. I knew that my grandmother took herself to bed grief-stricken, days before the priest arrived to tell her that her youngest son, Petsy, had been killed in the battle against the Japanese in Corregidor. She already knew. So I have always listened to my dreams, carefully. After my father died, my mother often asked if my father had appeared to me in my dreams. If I said yes, she'd ask, "How did he look? What did he say?" Once she dreamt she was riding a motorcycle and taking some hairpin turns. She leaned into them so much she landed on the floor and told me, "Your father was there when I picked myself up. He was laughing."

Several years after his death, she had dreamt that my father appeared at the door to our apartment with an unknown woman behind him. My mother began to get ready to go with him, but he said, "Not now. It's not time."

While at our cottage near the lake, a year before my mother's death, I had this dream:

We were in the living room of my mother's Florida apartment: my Aunt Helen, my mother's neighbors—Harriet, Nina, Ruthie—and I. My mother was in the center of the room inside a large structure shaped like a big egg or outdoor barbecue with an enormous curved top. She could open and close this lid at will. In the dream I knew that it was a coffin, and, when she closed the lid, it was her impending death that she did not want us to see.

In the middle of the night, I sat up, shuddering. Crying uncontrollably for some time, I finally woke Jack. I told him that I now knew my mother was going to die. "Your mother could live to be a hundred and five," he said. "She is not going to leave, yet."

But I knew what this dream meant. In the dream we were all at her house, so I assumed her death would take place on a holiday, a time when we were assembled in her living/dining room, together. For the next year, I dreaded each such event, anticipating the end.

But at the Bermuda Club that morning, after I landed from Chicago, they were all there as I had seen them in the dream—her neighbors (Nina, Harriet, Ruthie), Beatrice, and now me (not my Aunt Helen, gratefully; it would have been too hard for her). This was the scene—the one that would usher in her death. There was no large barbecue, no odd, pod-shaped vessel, of course, but my mother had hidden herself within the carapace of her strange behavior. She was trying to obscure what was happening. She was keeping it to herself, not allowing us to see what she must have known.

She was sitting halfway up on the rug when I arrived and was refusing to stand. I crouched down next to her and asked if she could get up. "Yes," she said, she could, but she was comfortable and did not want to. I was afraid to try to help her to stand. My mother was a large woman. Her friends were huddled together at the dining room table, crying. They had, of course, never seen her so vulnerable; for their sake, she pretended nothing odd was happening. Famously, she had been the one who had picked Pablo up off his kitchen floor, but that was long ago, when she still had her strength and balance. I called her doctor, weeping. He advised me to do something none of them wanted to do because it was against her wishes: "Call the paramedics."

When they came, she flirted with the young men and, with their help, she did get up and onto a stretcher. They took her to the hospital. She seemed coherent. Beatrice and I went with her, got her settled. They made us sit in the waiting area of the emergency room. While there, Beatrice insisted that I drive to my mother's lawyer and "get power of attorney." Beatrice understood the timeline we were now on.

Slight Detour

⁓

In the case of deep emotions, I have often felt that only part of me recognizes what is happening while it is happening. The rest remains hidden or, should I say, hiding, not ready for me to experience it—the truth—at least not all at once.

I reflect in amazement on all that I had to do in the months that followed. Had I thought earlier of any one of those actions in the abstract, it would have knocked me over. Instead I went to work, flew to Florida every week, made plans, and took care of logistics. I was not immobilized. I'm sure many look back on the preparation for profound loss with the same admiration for the self's ability to fragment itself long enough to get things done when all one really wants to do is dissolve.

In the emergency room, the nurses rehydrated her. We brought her a sandwich. If she could eat it and stand up, they said, she could go home. "But," they were emphatic, "she could no longer be left alone, at all." On the way out of the hospital, she noticed that it was a beautiful day. It was as if she had forgotten how lovely the air outside the air-conditioned apartment could be. I think of this often now, because I don't remember another day after that when we were out together and happy. Returning, she seemed so much like herself, so light of spirit for having been released from the dreaded hospital, relieved to be going home.

Fast-forward a few months. Beatrice is with her full-time now. Another caretaker, Elena, Beatrice's niece, also from Colombia, comes to sleep at the house at night. Although my mother seems comfortable with them both, she still insists that none of this is necessary. Her hearing now is so bad that she no longer picks up the phone. "How can I call you?" I ask her. "If they were not with you, I could not leave and go back to Chicago to work." She could no longer live alone.

The Hiatus

~

Somewhere between this moment and what was the beginning of the end, I had returned to Chicago. Things seemed stable in their impending instability. I thought there was time. For work I attended the Contemporary Art Biennale in Istanbul and then the Theatre Biennale in Venice—ten days. In Venice, I had gotten a call from Beatrice. My mother was in pain. It was unclear what it was, something in her back—a hairline fracture, perhaps. I can't remember all the conversations after that, only one with her doctor who called in the middle of the night, not realizing I was in Europe, in the days when few had international phones. I remember looking around that tiny room in Venice while we spoke—small, overstuffed velvet chairs, printed wallpaper, bedspreads with dancing women in ball gowns, all in deep reds, maroons, and white. I looked out the window into the darkness of the Venetian streets. "If it were a fracture, nothing could be done," he said. She was too old for surgery of any kind. We would just see. I gave permission to have her admitted to the hospital. Now I was in tears. I was so far away. What could I do from there? By the next day, she was stabilized. They thought perhaps the pain was kidney stones. She got better. She was eating. I breathed again.

By the time I returned to Chicago and then immediately to Florida, she was in rehab. When I saw her there, I was stunned. Why hadn't Beatrice told me she was doing so badly? She seemed unable to keep her eyes open. She wouldn't eat. She had been working with a physical therapist but was "without spirit," they said. "What can they do for her?" "Not much more," said the doctor, "unless her spirits pick up." "What would you do if she were your mother?" I asked the young doctor in her thirties. "I'd take her home," she said, "and I'd put her in hospice. If she wants to rally, she will. If not, then . . ."

I had to sit down. I was not prepared to hear this, but I was also not surprised. I asked my mother if she'd like to go home. "Can I?" she asked. I said, "You can, Mom, if you want to." "Then, yes, I would like to go home." The doctor wrote her diagnosis: "Failure to thrive." I had never heard of such a thing, but, of course, it was true. At this moment, at this juncture, she had failed to thrive. But she had thrived for ninety-seven years. "I've had a great life," she'd say. She had begun using that phrase some years ago. Whenever I heard it, I shuddered. She was done, I thought—summarizing—maybe staying just for me, because she knew I couldn't bear for her to go. She used to say to people, "Carol has no one," by which she meant no siblings. She thought that when she was gone, so was my family. Or maybe I was the excuse to stay, as she prepared herself to leave.

I met with the hospice people. It was the only way I could afford to take her home. Beatrice was relieved. She knew she could never take care of her alone. How would it work? "If your mother decides to thrive, then she'll simply stand up and go on with her life, but if she decides to let go, then she will be able to do so, and you will have helped to let that happen at home."

Thus, her slow exit began. Together, without saying a word, my mother and I had decided that she could leave her physical body, if she chose to. That's what I understood. And I believe she did as well.

Going Home

~

There were things I needed to do before they brought her to the apartment the next day. A hospital bed would have to be brought in. Would she mind? Oxygen and other equipment would be needed for the future. How could I make the house look normal and still accommodate all this stuff?

Alone, but with tenacity, I moved her bed—box spring and mattress—to the Bermuda Room, leaned it against the far wall, and prayed she wouldn't notice. When the hospital bed was installed, it was so much bigger and taller than her twin bed. But I put the same bedspread over it, although it barely fit, and hoped for the best. I was sure she'd comment on it. When she arrived and did not notice any of this, I knew she was adrift. The process had begun.

But that first weekend together was extraordinary for us. She was still able to walk to the bathroom herself, although I insisted she use the walker. I cooked dinner. She sat in the recliner chair that, after she slid off the couch, I had bought from one of Beatrice's former clients. It was higher and easier for her to get in and out of, and she could adjust it. We watched television.

I asked Beatrice to let us be alone for the weekend. Somehow, I knew this would be our last time alone. And, in all our life together, it turned out to be the closest. The struggle between us, the one I could never understand, was over. She was glad to be with me and I with her. Had it always been this way, we could have traveled together, enjoyed each other so much more.

I cooked tilapia and baked potatoes. Although she barely ate, she was so very glad to be home. I could see that she could hardly walk the few needed steps, even with the walker. Still, she seemed determined. The illusion she maintained, that she would get better and would need to be able to navigate herself, was still strong. But suddenly my mother seemed profoundly tired, as if the ninety-seven years had just caught up with her and all she wanted to do was sleep.

Many people were in and out that weekend. There were deliveries from hospice, yet she never asked about them. A very exuberant Cuban man came from the hospital with a new walker that suited her better. They talked. He also brought more oxygen. The home notary arrived, an enormous and gorgeous Caribbean woman with long dreads who made my mother laugh while getting her to sign all the powers of attorney. Harriet from next door on the right and Nina from next door on the left came to visit each day, as did her dear friend Ruthie each morning. Beatrice also came to say hello.

My mother seemed to perk up with all this energy around her. She could sit in the recliner and talk. It was almost normal.

I knew that she no longer really had control of her bowels. Beatrice had told me. She needed to wear special underwear. She had refused Beatrice's request many times, but she did not refuse me, and as I helped her to step into them, my heart sank. I knew my mother. If she were really conscious of what this meant, she would not do it, or having done it, she would leave. All of a sudden, the indignities were mounting. This she would not tolerate for long.

She had allowed herself to be brought home in a wheelchair, something she had always refused until that time. In the past, she would not have wanted anyone to see her unable to walk out of the elevator down the outside corridor to her apartment on her own. She had refused to walk with a cane and surely never with a walker, even in the apartment, although she was quite unsteady. But on this trip home, she did not care. She seemed not to notice anything in the outside world. And I guessed that she might never leave the apartment alive again. I knew this as they rolled her through the doorway. But none of it was ever discussed.

In the weeks that followed, my mother drifted in and out. She would sleep most of the day. At first we brought the television into the room, but she had no desire to watch it. She would often say to the women who came to care for her, "When I'm better, we'll go to lunch or I'll take you to dinner," as she always would have done in the past. She'd tell stories about her life, talk about my father and what a wonderful husband he had been. She was often very much herself, except that now she never left the bed. She took the care provided for granted. She never asked who these people were. The hospice nurses came each day. They changed her sheets, bathed her, rolling her from one side to the next, pulling the sheets and the garments out from under her and putting new ones on with such professional grace—all without moving her from the bed. They taught us how to do the same, but Beatrice and I were always reluctant, in part to protect my mother's privacy and in part because my mother was still a large woman and not easy to move.

But when I did help to sponge-bathe her, I was amazed that the skin protected from the sun on her large breasts, legs, and torso was like that of a young woman. She looked very beautiful to Beatrice and me, and we shared this appreciation of her. Ma Kali, often naked, yet they say, always "clad in space."[10]

We made sure that someone was constantly with her. Beatrice doing her word puzzles, me close to her, reading. "Why don't you go out? It's sunny today. You don't need to stay here," she'd say to me. "But I want to stay. I am happy to be with you." I was always glad to open the blinds in the morning, to surround her with light. Yet I knew that when I was not there, Beatrice always kept the blinds closed. She said the brightness hurt my mother's eyes. I also knew that had my mother cared either way, she would have spoken. There were times when she talked; at other times she was silent.

In the days when she was still speaking, she woke one afternoon and said, "I was dreaming we were moving—you, me, and Daddy. We were moving to a new home." I had had this same dream some nights before. In my dream, we were in Europe. My father was there, although I didn't see him. We were moving to another village. It was a transition. I was calm in the dream because we were all together.

One day she awoke and said to me, "There are many people coming in and out. I have money in my purse in the dresser. Take the money. Maybe it's not safe." "Mom, no one is going to steal your money," I said. "You don't know that," she said. "These people are strangers. Take the money." I went to her dresser and removed her bag from the drawer. I found $100. I told her the amount. "You see? There was a lot more." I doubted that there had been, but I could see that this situation agitated her. Even Beatrice, whom she saw every day, was unknown to her, new to the world of the past that she had now entered.

To give myself strength, each day I read from a Buddhist book called *Graceful Exits*.[11] It was filled with stories of monks and masters who had chosen their hour of death, predicted when, where, and how they would depart. Some had died lying down, others sitting or even standing, each story more inspirational and unimaginable than the next. If my mother and I could have talked about any of this, I might have read these stories to her, but we had not talked, could not talk about what was happening. Her mother had died at home. She, too, would die at home, which is what we both wanted, although it was never spoken.

I thought I remembered my Polish grandmother's death exactly as it was. But my cousin, who is five years older and lived in the house with my grandmother when this occurred, says my memory is wrong. Still, here is my version:

I was about six years old (she says I was younger). My beautiful, large Polish grandmother was in her bed, a white metal frame with a high, looped back, in an open, large, bright room. We had surrounded her bed. All my cousins were there—Cindy, Vince, Barbara, Essie. We were behind the headboard. My aunts and my mother were there, too, standing in front. The priest came. Everything was white except his black garments. She was silent, her eyes closed, her arms at her sides under starched sheets and blankets. It was winter. We had come to Pennsylvania to be with her. I remember that my younger cousins and I laughed inappropriately when the priest arrived. It was a strange scene for us, and, of course, children often respond to such reverent moments irreverently. I don't remember anything next, just the room: old, faded, light blue print wallpaper; a crucifix made of straw over her bed; a small, round mahogany night table with a cream-colored crocheted doily under a glass of water. The trap door that let the heat come into the room from the coal stove in the kitchen was open so people could come up and down the stairs and it would stay warm.

Perhaps I only dreamt it this way later. Who can be sure? I have learned now that my grandmother had ovarian cancer.

Her daughter-in-law, my Aunt Helen, cared for her magnificently.

The world is the producer of saintliness.[12]

My aunt had taken care of my grandmother and then later had done so much for my mother (although she was only a few years younger than my mother). Aunt Helen told me that one day my grandmother said to her in Polish, "I am getting my period again." My aunt had replied, "Mom, you can't be. You are eighty years old." But she was bleeding (metrorrhagia) and, of course, she was already very sick. Given the runoff from the coal mines and the water filled with sulfur in which we swam, and the rate of cancer in that small mining town, who knows what the cause of the illness might have been? She had given birth to ten children—so much could have gone wrong. In my memory, we were all around her, and she was leaving us.

This is how I always believed one should die—at home with those who love you best. Having had this image for most of my life, I wanted my mother to be surrounded by this same quiet sense of devotion, to know she had been loved, still was loved, and was having a dignified, safe, death—and that we would do anything to make this possible.

I didn't know enough to protect my father in this way. He had had quadruple bypass surgery and, although he made it through the operation, all his systems had broken down. When it was clear he would not survive, he was already in the clutches of the hospital. Plugged into so many systems, we could not have moved him. My mother was too emotional. She couldn't be with him at the end. When she would walk into his room, she would collapse. I'd have to insist she wait outside. Her sobbing agitated him too much, and he was on a ventilator and could not speak. We had neither the clarity nor the courage to take him off dialysis. That was twenty years before.

The same would not happen to my mother.

But in the middle of her glacially slow, contemplative death, came the hurricane.

III

WATER: THE STORM

Man only escapes from the laws of the world in lightning flashes. Instants when everything stands still. . . .[13]

In the more than twenty-five years that my mother lived in Florida, her home had never been hit by a hurricane. Many had come and gone, some catastrophic like Hurricane Andrew in 1992, turning houses into toothpicks, but such annihilating storms had never landed on Tamarac. Nonetheless, my mother was always ready with several plastic gallons of water, the bathtub filled, and a flashlight in the kitchen.

But in mid-October of 2005, a series of newscasts began to track a very powerful hurricane on its way from Cape Verde to southern Florida. This was Wilma, and it turned out to be one of the most destructive hurricanes in Florida's history. Broward County was predicted to be its epicenter, the place where the eye of the storm would touch down. It was a location already ridiculously famous for the "hanging chad" fiasco during the first election of George W. Bush. It also was the county of the Bermuda Club and, for me at the time, the omphalos of the cosmos.

I had to return to Chicago for three days but planned to get back before the storm hit. Flights to Fort Lauderdale, usually overbooked, were empty. Almost no one but me was on board, except for a few totally deranged vacationers who still believed their cruises might sail or that their flights to the islands might "go." Even the flight attendants wanted to be somewhere else other than on that early United Airlines flight heading into the storm and they planned to turn around and fly right back north after we landed.

The prediction was that in two days Hurricane Wilma would land in the Gulf of Mexico, then would make its way across to Florida. My goal was to be there with my mother when the storm hit and also to help prepare us all for what it might bring. When we landed, the airport was full of frenetic people trying to fly out. For me, all space was contracting to one location—the bed where my mother was dying.

When I arrived at the Bermuda Club, my mother was asleep, as she almost always was these days. I told Beatrice to stay with her while I went to stock up. I had read the papers. The supposed worst case: no potable water for some time, no electricity for a day or two, all flights cancelled, and so forth. I bought more water jugs, larger flashlights, and a hand-cranked radio. I loaded the refrigerator with lots of food (not really imagining what would happen if there were no electricity for an extended time), filled the rental car with gas, and waited.

The air was thick with humidity but also with fear. Grown children were arriving to get their parents out. For us there was nowhere to go. I checked on our neighbors, made sure they, too, were ready. Really, though, how could they be? Paul next door could not walk. Gloria's husband downstairs was bedridden. My mother was, well, asleep and dying. There was a lot of anticipation and speculation. What would we do if we had to be evacuated? It was too much to imagine. So we went on as always, waiting.

We must believe in the reality of time. Otherwise, we are in a dream.[14]

I had never anticipated a storm before. The raging hurricanes that came to New Jersey in those pre-media summers, when my father ran the auction room on the boardwalk in Point Pleasant, just arrived. I don't remember waiting for them. But when they arrived, they rocked the foundation of the old clapboard rooming house where we stayed to its core. My father loved Babe, the owner—a tough, bony, white-haired woman who had seen many storms. "Babe's" was just feet from the boardwalk, so when the rains came, they came. We locked the shutters and hoped for the best, then spent the next days wading through debris. But this was something else. The quiet we maintained in the house for my mother and the fury that we were anticipating outside made the apartment feel that it could buckle into itself from the conflicting forces. I had to remember to breathe.

On the evening of the storm, I was alone with my mother. Beatrice and Elena were both too worried about their own apartments to be absent from them, so I was on watch. When this was the case, I would sleep on an air mattress at the entrance to my mother's room, so that I would hear if she needed anything. I could never bring myself to sleep on the other twin bed in her room that once had been my father's and then became my Aunt Helen's when she stayed with my mother for the winter months. It seemed too intimate, too invasive to simply move in, and my mother now made so many noises during the night, slept so fitfully, that it was hard for anyone to sleep too near to her. Even in the living room, at the entrance to her bedroom, on that rubber inflatable bed, I was up most of the night.

The evening of the hurricane was no different. It started quietly. I had cooked a chicken soup, but my mother could not eat. She had asked for ginger ale, but could not drink more than a spoonful. She was failing, fading, but her heart and lungs were still strong. Her body seemed now to be willfully starving itself so that she could leave. It was as they had said—if she wanted to rally, she would. She did not. Yet she seemed so good-spirited, never complained, always said what wonderful care she was receiving, now still talking, although not much.

On this night awaiting the storm, I woke every hour. Finally, about 2 a.m., I could hear the wind hurtling itself through the palms, and the rain began. At first it seemed innocent enough—just a big storm but manageable. Soon, however, the wind was howling. I touched the windows, and they were vibrating. What if they shattered? I had never thought of this. If the big window next to my mother's bed buckled in the middle of the night, what would I do? I could not move her. She could not move herself. The bed weighed a ton. I stared out the window and saw the bending trees and torrential rain, heard the howling accelerate. Through the kitchen window, I watched a hinged cast-iron gate—the extravagant entrance to the new assisted-living complex across the road—skid down the street like a paper plane. I watched a telephone pole do the same. And then a large streetlamp, yanked right out of the ground, joined these other massive objects careening down the main road. A stray electrical wire hit the side of a telephone pole. Massive sparks illuminated the ground for a second, then the streetlights—which had shone into my mother's kitchen window for twenty years—went dark.

By then I was praying, my version: *"Absolutely unmixed attention is prayer."*[15] And I was asking, "Please don't let the windows snap. I will not know how to protect her. Let her die in peace." In the middle of this, while watching the trees surrounding the Bermuda Club flying uprooted in the air, my mother, who could hear very little anyway and only when she really paid attention, woke up and asked, "Is it raining?" This made me laugh. "Mom, it's not raining. It's beyond raining…." I could barely speak. "The gates have been ripped up, trees have fallen on cars, telephone poles are sliding down the street. Mom, it's a massive hurricane." To which she replied, "Really? Well then, honey, I'm glad I'm in bed," and fell back to sleep.

This is how it would be, now and forever. My once-powerful mother could no longer protect herself, or me. I was alone.

I watched from her windows as the Bermuda Club itself was nearly swept into the sea, like Eden, lost to us forever in the eleventh book of Milton's *Paradise Lost*.

> *Then shall this mount*
> *Of Paradise by might of waves be moved*
> *Out of his place, pushed by the horned Flood*
> *With all his verdure spoiled and trees adrift*
> *Down the great River to the op'ning gulf*
> *And there take root an island salt and bare,*
> *The haunt of seals and orcs and sea-mews' clang,*
> *To teach thee that God attributes to place*
> *No sanctity if none be thither brought. . . .* [16]

The Wake

~

Early the next morning, Beatrice arrived. She had walked around the corner from her building to announce that her car was lodged under massive tree branches and could not be moved. There was flooding all around her building, live wires were buried in its depths, and she, too, had no electricity. How would she manage? How would we? "Hour by hour," I said. What else could we do?

I asked her to stay with my sleeping mother while I walked around the complex to see what I could learn. Many of the extravagantly wide banyan trees that encircled the Bermuda Club had been toppled, some now resting on cars. My rental car was clear of debris. I was lucky, but other cars were smashed irreparably, windshields shattered. People were dazed and incredulous, wrack and rubble everywhere. Some were crying. At the clubhouse, the large metal canopy that protected us from the sun was now in the pool, along with all the large stationary umbrellas. (Why hadn't anyone removed them before it began?) Chairs and tables were draped on the tops of surrounding fences as if giants had come in the night, used them to play bocce ball, and then thrown them into the air to land randomly.

I decided to walk up to the small cluster of stores on Commercial Boulevard to see if anything was open. En route I met a distraught woman in a pink housecoat. "I've lost my porch," she said, "I can't find my porch." Her stucco bungalow now had an enormous rent where once a porch had been. I searched with her for a while, but we could not find it. Where might such a heavy, cumbersome thing have blown? Several shop owners were standing by their store entrances unable to open the metal electrical gates that closed over the glass at night. These gates were designed to open only from an inside switch. Without electricity, they would remain shut for weeks. Some had managed to roll theirs up a bit from the bottom, but once inside, all was dark. We all wanted to normalize our situation, to return to life as it had been, but that was a long way off.

The lack of electricity posed difficulties I could not have imagined. No one in my mother's complex had refrigeration. Most had no phones. Everything dependent on electricity was stalled. Portable phones no longer worked, and people could not charge their cells. Because my mother had refused to upgrade her phone, we still had a heavy, clunky, cream-colored landline model that miraculously worked. We thus became phone central for her building.

The elevator, essential for everyone over eighty, did not function, so most residents were unable to get down from their apartments—or up to them. Gloria's husband was stuck in his hospital bed, which could not be moved out of its raised position. We also could not adjust my mother's bed. Amazingly, the hospice nurse got to us that day and said she'd try to find the crank, but she called later to say that the warehouse, where such things were kept, was inaccessible because its electrical door could not be opened.

Gas could not be pumped, so people with empty tanks were unable to drive. But driving was impossible anyway, because whole trees, roofs, and wires were littering the road. There were no working streetlights, creating chaos for those who tried. And there were those insanely determined drivers who, even in this early hour of the first day, were pulling branches off the roads, determined to get somewhere, anywhere, by car.

I was very worried about Rose—one of my older friends, the mother of a colleague from Chicago—who just happened also to live in the Bermuda Club. She had survived Auschwitz and, I thought, could probably endure a hurricane and its aftermath, but she, too, had become increasingly fragile. And I imagined that she had been up all night.

Had the phones been working, I would have called first, as I always did. Instead, I just walked over. No doorbells were working, so I knocked loudly and yelled her name and mine, so she wouldn't be afraid.

When Rose finally heard me and opened the door, I immediately saw that she was a wreck. Her hair, normally so well coiffed, was standing on end, and she had panic in her eyes. "Come in. Sit down. Eat. I'm making lunch." Once inside, she was trying to balance on a small stepladder, straining to reach into the cabinet for a can of tuna. She was very small and her body, twisted from her time in the camps, was also very shaky. The ladder, too, was quivering. I asked her to please let me help. With uncommon abruptness, she said, "Sit. You sit. *Sit*." Rose was distraught. It was all too much. Everything was quickly going to turn bad without refrigeration, including her insulin. She could not walk up and down the stairs from the third floor. She could not go shopping. And although her children had bought her a cell phone for such occurrences, she did not know how to use it and, anyway, had left it sitting in a drawer for months so it was out of juice. She could not call.

I didn't want to eat, but I could see there was no refusing Rose. The world had turned upside down, and she was trying to make it normal. But she looked wild and almost pushed me back into my seat when I stood up. This was not good. "Rose, can I get you anything?" I asked before leaving, seeing her calm down a bit. "I'd love a hot cup of tea," she answered. I said I'd try, but I knew this would be impossible.

Rose was out of body, and she could not stay in her apartment alone for long. I ate what she put before me, walked home, and called Daniel, her son. I told him that no matter how much she protested, he had to get her out of her condo. Anyone who was not in Broward County on that day could not visualize the damage, could not imagine what it might have set off emotionally for that generation of Jews who had already lived through the war, the camps, the losses, and now were too old and helpless to deal with such an event. The next day one of her children's in-laws came from Boca Raton and took her to their house for what became the next three weeks.

As it turned out, the hurricane didn't just mark the impending end of my mother's life. It marked the end of a collective delusion that moving to Florida for one's later years would be a safe alternative to New York winters. It showed parents and their grown children that a warm and seemingly hospitable place quickly could become a nightmare as relatives up north tried to reach those down south but could not, and as parents and grandparents attempted to get out of Florida to their children up north, but could not. Why had anyone ever thought that living far from your family when you were old and most vulnerable was a good idea?

My mother's friend Ruthie, who lived two buildings over, had lost the roof of her entire building, and rain had seeped into all the apartments, even hers on the ground floor. She could not stay there any longer. Although my mother was her closest friend, she would not accept my invitation to come live with us. It was too painful for her to see my mother dying. Ruthie did not have her apartment back for a year. In the long run, the damage and devastation meant that almost no one could sell their apartments for a decade to come. The investment that was to be their "nest egg" became a burden overnight.

It seems impossible that this is true, but we did not have electricity for two weeks. The days were almost normal (as normal as our life now could be). But the nights felt interminably long as I sat with my mother, trying to read by flashlight, the room illuminated by candlelight. Beatrice would leave when it started getting dark, fearful of walking around the corner alone to her apartment because there had been vandals.

When my mother would awaken, I'd try to explain what was happening and to get her to drink or eat something. People came in and out to use the phone. Without warm water, it was hard to bathe her; we did our best. The hospice nurses were resourceful. Miraculously, one day one arrived with the crank so we could finally lower the top half of her bed. We hoped it would make her more comfortable, but she didn't seem to notice.

In the midst of all of this, I had to go back to Chicago to make a legal deposition about a faculty tenure case. It was essential that I do this, and I was on the phone endlessly (thank God we had a phone) with Rich, my travel agent of many years, trying to figure out from which airport I could leave and to which one I could return.

We figured that if I could get to Orlando, which had not been hit by Wilma, I could fly out. I had a full tank of gas, and it was a two-hour drive. In normal conditions, it would definitely work. But who knew what the roads would be like? I did a trial run to the freeway, even though there were no stoplights and hence a great deal of turmoil. The lines for gas were around the block for the one station that could still pump. Cars waiting to get in line were all over the roads in random places. Cars also were backed up on the freeway, trying to get around other cars that had been abandoned when they ran out of gas. It was as if a war attack had come and gone, and the survivors were desperately trying to get out before a second took place.

On the morning I had to leave, I got up very early. Beatrice came. I kissed my sleeping mother and prayed that I'd make it to Chicago and back while she was still alive. I had multiple anxiety attacks while driving and called my agent from my depleting cell phone more than once, asking if he thought I should turn back. I feared I'd run out of gas because the roads were jammed and the trip was taking so much longer than we had calculated. He kept urging me forward and, miraculously, I made it to Orlando. But when I got there and went to drop off the car, I realized that no one in Orlando seemed to know anything about what had happened only two hours away in Broward County. Incredulous, I was a survivor talking about the devastation I just had left, but no one understood.

I must have looked very rattled because the attendant at the United Airlines desk was very sympathetic when she heard my story and upgraded me to first class. I was grateful. I needed a gift.

The long line through security was populated by children with Mickey Mouse ears and adults in Donald Duck T-shirts, all returning from Disney World's Epcot Center. Reality couldn't have looked more fun-filled and rosy to them. Their obliviousness made me shudder.

I landed in Chicago at night, went home, and called Beatrice. Nothing had changed. I slept deeply and the next morning went in to speak with the committee that was hearing the tenure case. I consulted with our lawyers, gave my testimony with passion and conviction. The lawyer bringing the case against the school quit when he heard the logic behind our testimonies. Done. I got on the subway, went to O'Hare, flew back to Orlando, rented a car, drove back to Fort Lauderdale, and was with my mother again, a day later.

That night, Beatrice asked me how long I thought my mother would last. One week? Two? More? Although I had read the hospice literature, I was totally unprepared to answer the question and surprised she had asked. At this point, my mother was virtually starving herself, but this was part of the predicted "failure to thrive" scenario.

In the meantime, my mother would speak from time to time. She asked for Jack, and I called and told him to come to Florida immediately. One day she said to me, "You look just like Grandma Becker." I was taken aback since my grandmother, whom I adored, was nonetheless very small and very round. I feared I looked like her to my mother. But then she said, "She was a wonderful person." I knew my mother really meant this and soon realized it was her way of saying that I was a wonderful person, a statement that never could have come from her to me directly. Grateful, I started to cry and left the room.

In the middle of this mayhem, the last wisp of ice that I often felt between us melted. As an adult the only other time I had felt this clarity of closeness with her was when my father was dying. I had brought a bottle of Krupnik —Polish honey liquor—with me from my Ukrainian neighborhood in Chicago. Every night, after returning from the hospital, she and I would each have a shot of Krupnik in tea. Losing the great love we shared, there was no fight left in either of us.

It had never been a question of devotion between my mother and me. That was unconditional. But it had not been easy or comfortable. Perhaps it was always about my father—our mutual, deep attachment to him. Or perhaps I had become "Other" to her, educated beyond her, living a life to which she had no access. Perhaps this made her insecure or jealous. I never knew, will never know, and no longer care. Amazingly, there we were, working together, focused on the joint task of carrying out her death. That was all there was.

On another evening she woke from her interminable sleep and said, "What are we making for the dinner party?" I realized she was in a dream state or hallucinating, but since cooking and food were often what we talked about, I was comforted by the familiar discourse. "What would you like us to serve?" I asked. "How about salmon?" I offered. "Good.

And what else?" she said. "How about green beans, oven po-tatoes?" I suggested. "There will be a lot of people," she said. Then I said, "What about adding chicken too—Greek style?" (She liked that. She had worked for Greeks her whole life.) We continued in this way until she drifted back to sleep. She was seeing a party to come and thinking, as we often did together, how to be good hosts.

By this time two weeks had passed since the storm and there were still no streetlights, but electricity had returned and, with it, our house lights and hot water. We washed my mother's hair and put her in a new dressing gown so that she could receive Jack at her best. I knew this would be important to her.

Jack arrived on a Friday late afternoon. When my mother saw him and then the two of us together, she exclaimed to Beatrice, "Don't they look beautiful?"

Then, as we each stood on opposite sides of her bed, she said, "You two should get married." Since she had never said this before, or anything like it, I knew she was thinking that she would be gone soon and I should have a husband. I would need one. She had told Loretta, one of her caregivers years before, that she worried that when she was no longer here, I'd "have no one." This pained me. Although I am an only child, I've always had many deep friendships. Several women are like sisters, some men like brothers—our friendships have been strong for decades. She knew them all. And, of course, there was Jack and his son and daughter-in-law, also very close to me. I was sorry she felt there would be "no one," but it was her way of worrying and perhaps expressing her guilt that I had no siblings. There were ten children in her family—for her, that was how it should be.

Jack and I looked at each other across her bed, and we knew that we would get married. Why not? It was her wish and, as it turns out, her last. She said one last thing to Jack: "I love you, and my mother loves you." Leaving us now, she was already in conversation with her mother—my Grandmother Catherine—and, I assumed, her brothers, sisters, and friends, all waiting on the other side. She did not speak to us again after that day.

What to Say/Who Should Say It

We must not seek the void, for it would be tempting God if we counted on supernatural bread to fill it. We must not run away from it either.[17]

In anticipating my mother's imminent departure and the moments right after and before the Neptune Society would arrive to take her, I tried to envision a small, spiritual service.

Because my mother was not Jewish, a rabbi would make no sense to her. Anyway, we didn't know any in Florida whom we liked. Should there be a priest? I remembered my mother and aunt livid in front of the television set right after one of the many Catholic Church pedophile scandals. "Those guys are all sick," my mother said. "They should close down all the parochial schools." She surely was not sentimental about the Church. Maybe not a priest.

I remembered reading that hospice could provide a member of the clergy who could be at your home at the time of death. I called and explained the situation. The next day a Unitarian minister came to meet me at the apartment. He was nice enough, young, but all too quickly was telling me his problems: "I don't really want to be in the ministry anymore. I was thinking of going back to school and getting a degree in literature. You're a professor. What do you think?" I was soon giving him career advice and deciding, quietly, that he was not the presence I hoped to find for her. He went in to meet my mother. She opened her eyes for him, graciously, as he touched her hand. Not him, I thought. No gravitas.

I called hospice back. I asked if they had a Buddhist monk or teacher they could send. They said they did and would call me back. Time was crushing in, and I was becoming more and more anxious. Jack and I had gone to Borders bookstore, bought a Bible and an edition of Roethke poems: "I learned not to fear infinity / The far field, the windy cliffs of forever."[18] I wanted Jack to read something, and Beatrice, too, if she were present. I wanted to sing the *Prajnaparamita*—the Heart Sutra—for my mother. It had been integral to my own Buddhist studies. My mother would have been surprised to hear it, but I knew she would not mind. It is calming, and it is the sutra to help free people from the rounds of birth and death. "Form is emptiness: Emptiness form."[19] The order was becoming clearer.

The Buddhist monk called back. She was gentle, smart, and knowledgeable—everything I'd hoped for, but she lived quite far away. It seemed unlikely that, at the moment of my mother's death, she could race over and be with us. But we talked for quite a while. She finally said, "You can do this yourself. You don't need anyone. You know what you want to say. You can lead."

On the morning my mother died, the monk called, having seen a notation in the hospice report for the day. She had offered the spiritual guidance I needed. She had given me courage.

The Neighbors

Very close to the end, my mother's friend and neighbor Greta called. Could I come over that evening? She wanted to talk. I assumed she was concerned about us and also felt that time was moving quickly.

When I entered her apartment, she was finishing an enormous jigsaw puzzle of Versailles. The pieces took up most of the dining room table.

"Carol," she said, "I need to ask you about something. Last year you bought your mother the same dinette set that I have. See mine here in the kitchen? When your mother dies, could I have the chairs to hers? Mine are all shot, and they look bad. I could take them now if you don't mind."

Stunned, I said, "Greta, I am not ready to talk about the apartment or the dinette chairs, not ready to dismantle her—

our—life here yet. But, if you insist, you can have the set and anything else you'd like once I sell the apartment, but not now and not until then. I will want to have furniture in the apartment when people come to see it."

"But look at me," she said, "I'm sitting on this bad chair with a loose back. It's hurting me. Your mother won't notice anymore. She doesn't get out of bed. She's not using the chairs. What's the difference if you give them to me now or later? I'm asking before Harriet does. She has the same set and the same problem. The chairs have fallen apart, and the ones you bought your mother are new."

Stunned again. "Well, why don't you bring one of your perfectly good dining room chairs into the kitchen until I can give you the others and not sit on a broken chair?

"Because, as you can see, a chair from the dining room won't match the dinette set. It won't look good."

"But who will see?" I said. "Who will care?"

"I will care," she said. I promised again that after my mother was gone, after the apartment was sold, she could have the whole set. I said goodnight and left, sick in heart and, finally, just amused.

Time and Space Converging

In the inner life, time takes the place of space.[20]

That night, the breathing became worse, the wheezing had begun. It was getting very close. When my Aunt Harriet died, soon after my father, she was at home in hospice, too. My mother and I were there when she made the sound. "That's the death rattle," my mother said. I had not heard it before. Now I was praying to my Grandmother Catherine, my mother's mother: Please take her. She's suffering.

The death agony is the supreme dark night which is necessary even for the perfect, if they are to attain to absolute purity and for that reason it is better that it should be bitter.[21]

I had always thought my mother would slip away gently. That was not the case.

At 2 a.m., I went to bed, desperate to sleep. Elena was with her, trying to sleep on the mattress near her bed. She knocked on my door at 6 a.m. "Your mother is very bad." She had propped her up a bit to make the breathing easier. She had given her more morphine drops. I had begged them repeatedly not to sedate her more than necessary, just to help her if she was suffering, but nothing to make her sleep. I challenged hospice on this: Why would you drug her to sleep when all she did was sleep? Until this time, she had only ever taken an aspirin. I had seen that glassy and beseeching look in her eyes when I'd last come from Chicago—too much sedation. She did not need this. Not now. Not when her consciousness should be most clear.

But she was gasping, breathing hard. *"Body from spirit slowly does unwind."*[22]

I called hospice. I needed their help. By the time they arrived, it was almost over. When everyone left the room for a moment, my mother opened her eyes, looked straight at me, took her last breath, and was gone. Beatrice and Elena came in. The hospice nurses came in. We put her teeth back into her mouth and we tied a scarf up around her head to hold them in place. I knew she would not want to leave the apartment without them. We washed her body. And then I asked everyone to leave us alone.

I sat with her, sang to her, held her hand. I cried, talked, laughed about George, whom we both had loved so much, thanked her for all she had given me—her good health, her strong body, her confidence. I don't know how long I sat there, but it was long enough to feel her hand grow cold and to see her coloring change, a translucent blueness take over the skin. I prayed that the spirit had left unencumbered.

I then asked Jack, Beatrice, and Elena to come in and I sang the Heart Sutra. We then all read to her, passages each had chosen. I asked everyone to stay calm, very calm. We wanted to send her off peacefully. We did not want to clutch. We did not want to show her our pain. We wanted her spirit to fly away free of us and from the body that had been so powerful and grounded to the earth her whole life but now had become so very tired.

While all this was happening, I could hear the hospice worker outside, talking on her cell phone. I was sure she was calling all this in to the office, but, nonetheless, I wanted her to stop. I didn't want that chatter anywhere around us. We had protected the space so fiercely for these months.

After some time, I called the Neptune Society. They would come shortly. No rush. Please don't rush. I was so reluctant to let her go but also knew she would not want us to keep her in this state for too long.

When they arrived, I was surprised that their emissaries were such young men—boys, really—in white shirts and black pants. I said that my mother was heavy, although much less than she had been, and asked if they could handle her. They said they would bring a stretcher.

Jack told me later that one of the young men waited on the catwalk while the other went to the van. He returned with a not-so-clean-looking sheet, and the older boy said, "Not that one. The velvet one, stupid."

They arrived with a stretcher and a lush, deep red cloth. They wrapped my mother in this fabric, except for her face, and, as they were leaving, I asked Jack to bring some cash. It just occurred to me that my mother would want to give them something for this difficult task. I stood with my hands in a prayer pose as they stopped in the living room. I asked them each to take this as a gift from us that my mother would have wanted them to have. I said my parents always had been generous and that this small gesture would matter to my mother. The hospice worker told me not to make jokes when I was upset. I told her that this was not a joke but rather how my mother would have wanted us to be with these young men.

My mother would have understood, immediately, that they were out of their depth, yet trying to get it right.

And now that my physical mother was gone, I sat on the couch doubled over in pain, as if I had been punched in the stomach—something my cousin Mark used to do to me when we were kids. I hadn't experienced such an abrupt loss of breath since that time.

Prasada

~

In the temples dedicated to the Goddess Kali, a great deal of the rituals involve the preparation of the food that will be offered to the goddess. After the food has been presented to the altar, and the goddess has had her chance to eat her fill, the offering is divided among her devotees. The food that has been offered, and is now to be eaten by the devotees, is called Prasad—which means a generous gift. It is said that the gods do not eat as we know it, but their presence changes the essential structure of the food. It transforms it from food essential to the body to food essential to the spirit. Devotees come from great distances for this special sustenance.[23]

That night I invited all my mother's friends for dinner—Chinese carry-out in her apartment. I could think of nothing they liked more.

We ordered all their favorites and hers—chow mein, moo shu pork, wonton soup, chicken fried rice—food they all enjoyed, although the Fort Lauderdale version wasn't very good.

But her friends never seemed to mind. It was always a treat for them. Perhaps over the years away from New York, they all, even my mother, had forgotten how good Chinese food could be.

There had been so many Sundays in my New York childhood when we went to Chinatown to eat at Sam Woo's or another nondescript, small restaurant that someone had recommended or that my parents had happened upon—one that made the best spare ribs or moo goo gai pan. We'd meet their friends there, often in a large group, and order many dishes. When it was over, we'd walk to Little Italy for cannoli at Ferrari's. That's what Sunday always was. I also enjoyed all those touristy stores—the talking fortune chickens and plastic replicas of the Statue of Liberty that glowed in the dark, clamshells that flowered in water, and whole cities that grew from a small pink pill overnight.

I set the table with the best crystal, porcelain plates, and a real linen tablecloth—all the things from my mother's reserve that we used to use all the time in New York and had left untouched these last years. Her very close friends arrived, all dressed up. We felt her spirit around us, and I knew, for them, her strength had been an anchor, and I hoped it would be still.

Later, I set out all the beautiful antique cups and saucers that filled our credenza. I then asked each of them to choose a set and to use it for tea, as my mother would have wanted them to do. "What are you saving them for? Use them," she would have said. "So what if they break. Who cares?" There were always more. We had boxes of wonderful things that my father had brought from his life as an auctioneer, carting precious objects from towns like Hackensack and Poughkeepsie. What would become of all this now?

A Month Later

~

In Chicago I orchestrated the dinner that my mother had seen in her reverie and tried to plan with me before she left— a party in her honor but for all my friends. I had made the dining room table into an altar alight with candles for the occasion and photos of my mother surrounded by the flowers people had brought or sent. She looked beautiful in all the images, even the most recent, taken when she was ninety-seven. There was my mother in the 1930s, wearing a fabulous coat with an enormous ermine collar, her hair swept up with a big tortoise-shell comb, her profile like Carole Lombard's. There she was wading in a dam in Hastings, Pennsylvania, wearing loose Katharine Hepburn–style pants rolled up, or sitting on the bank of a river, holding a fishing pole, looking straight ahead to the water, wearing a very smart, small beret, my Aunt Helen on her right side, with thick auburn hair, leaning in toward the camera. And there was my father and mother snuggling in a booth at some New York nightclub— he in his army uniform, she with a large corsage on her lapel, my mother smiling and looking straight at the camera, my father squinting in the bright lights.

For this dinner I ordered from Artopolis: baked salmon, Greek roasted chicken, potatoes *al forno* with lots of olive oil and onions. I made a huge salad and ordered a big choco-late cake. There was plenty of food, just as she would have wanted it. The Polish equation—at least three times as much as needed.

My closest friends came. We said *Kaddish*. We drank. We made toasts. It was the party she saw, the one she wanted, more for me than for herself (I am sure), but nonetheless a party with life and love. My Polish cousins—her nieces—came from the South Side with their husbands.

It was the send-off I could not pull off in Florida because so few of her close friends and family were still alive. The last thing I had wanted was an empty funeral home in Broward County. In Chicago, it was joyful and tearful and exactly as she had dreamt it. We—she and I—always had lots of people for dinner, but this time we gathered to say good-bye.

Taking Stock

~

When I left my mother's apartment to return to Chicago, I simply closed the door. It was all I could manage at the time. There even were moments when I thought of keeping the apartment, but her lawyer with the green 1950s cat's-eye, rhinestone glasses, so tough and so right, had said, "Don't keep the apartment for sentimental reasons. It will be a bur-den. Once you are officially the owner, the next tax assess-ments will go way up. Your mother was so old. She was in a special category. But they'll kill you. Sell the apartment." I never could imagine coming down with Jack and staying there anyway. It would have been too lonely, too sad. It was my mother's life, and she had lived it well. She had felt safe there, even in the end. Luckily, she never had to see the Bermuda Club decimated by the hurricane.

After this, there were several return trips. The first one was to retrieve the ashes, when I brought Lisa to the house to meet my mother's friends. That time, it was as if she were still there—nothing had changed. The lawyer had asked for the original will. I thought that I had given it to her, but, when I went to find it in the apartment, I was steered right to it—my mother's presence and guidance still so strong.

Everything in the apartment was intact: the worn, fake-lace plastic tablecloth, the black, wrought-iron, Tiffany-style shade with blue glass that hung in the dining room (an inexplicable narrative of horse-drawn coaches and women in ballroom dresses, always a dreamy landscape to me, etched into the glass). There was the big credenza with all the objects that she had saved, those that had made the cut—the ones she did not give away when they left Brooklyn, the crème de la crème. There were ruby-colored, thin-stemmed wine glasses that had once belonged to my Jewish grandmother and crystal bowls that my father had found in "stocks"; the large fish platter that belonged to Grandma Becker with images of swimming trout in various shades of green and cattails painted along the sides; the golden-colored glass pitcher with four fluted glasses that my mother had once tried to send to me in Chicago via UPS but had been told by the young agents working there that they could not take responsibility for things so delicate and so old, thus had remained in Florida. I saw the many China cups with delicate flower patterns and saucers to match (like those I had offered to her friends) and the strange Hummel figurines of little boys fishing and little girls on mushrooms contemplating something—their index fingers thoughtfully posed against their cheeks. (My mother, sensing my disdain for these, always insisted I take them back to Chicago.) And there were soup terrines in diaphanous white porcelain with forest green trim and huge matching ladles. These were objects we hardly ever used; still, they had always been in our lives. Except for the egregious Hummel figurines, they are all smothered in bubble wrap, stored, perhaps forever, in a locker on Clybourn Street in Chicago.

Selling the Apartment

~

After the hurricane, there were at least seventy apartments on the market at the Bermuda Club. With Nina's help, however, I found a realtor willing to take on ours. I was almost ready to give it away, but I knew I shouldn't do that. If we went too low, it would skew the market for others who really needed to recoup their investment. But because of the glut of apartments for sale, many with new kitchens and other renovations, I feared we'd never sell ours. So we went low enough to put us about twenty-fifth on the "for sale" list. Months went by; I was too busy to focus on it. There were nibbles, but no serious activity.

That October, I returned to Laos for *The Quiet in the Land*, an extensive art project in which I had been involved with my friend—curator France Morin—and others for some time. During this visit to Luang Prabang, I was sleeping in a guesthouse next to a lagoon covered with algae. It was a dreamy place (albeit a bit moldy). But since one always dreams deeply when on a lagoon, dream I did—another auditory dream. It communicated this simple thought: "You will sell the house."

I now knew my mother was on it. The last thing she would have wanted was for me to be stuck with her apartment. I was relieved and completely convinced that it would be sold.

I was back only a week when the agent called. He had a buyer, a "live one." How low would I go? He recommended dropping the price $5,000, to what the buyer was offering. That would allow her to pay the closing fees and so forth. If this would do it, then yes, I'd drop the price. And so the sale process began. Forms were faxed back and forth, but I would have to go to Florida for the closing. The realtor said, "Don't worry about the furniture. I know a Haitian Goodwill with a truck that will come and take it all. They won't be able to give you official forms for a tax write-off, but they'll take everything you leave for free, and you won't be bothered."

I came back to Fort Lauderdale to sign the papers, my heart dropping as it always did when I got anywhere near the Fort Lauderdale airport. But, as always, her friends were waiting to see me, the house was full of light, and even then, with so much already sent north, it still was her house, furnished as it had always been, a place my mother had truly loved.

I asked all her friends to come over. I knew that Elena wanted the couch (the new couch I had bought my mother, hiding the price tag until the end). Allison, the Jamaican woman who cared for Paul next door, wanted the lamps. Beatrice, who had given my mother such steadiness during those last months, wanted the recliner she had helped me buy from her former client. Greta, of course, got all the dinette chairs (complaining until the end that she had had to wait so long). I gave away all I could to those who had been close. The rest, the realtor promised, would be carted off by the "Haitian Goodwillers," whose "truck had broken down but who, nevertheless, would get there in the next days." I was "not to worry." And so I didn't. I slept for the last time in the guest room on that dreadfully uncomfortable convertible sofa (reminiscent of my Crown Heights childhood) and looked through my father's tools and other objects once more. Jack came down so we could pack all the rest. In the morning, we took the rental car and drove from the Bermuda Club to the airport. I cried the whole way. When I said good-bye to everyone, I promised to return. And I did, but only once. After that, I could not.

It turned out that the Haitian Goodwill was a fabrication. The Cuban woman who moved into the apartment (the mother of the couple who bought it for her) was upset with the realtor, who apparently had promised "all the furniture." Perhaps she had paid the realtor something for what, in the end, she did not get. That would explain why she was surprised when the couch disappeared. This, of course, I learned from the neighbors.

IV

AIR: GRACE

All the natural movements of the soul are controlled by laws analogous to those of physical gravity. Grace is the only exception.[24]

Recalling these lines from Samuel Beckett's *Waiting for Godot*, I would like to talk about how my mother and I have communicated since her death:

> **Estragon:** All the dead voices.
>
> **Vladimir:** They make a noise like wings.
>
> **Estragon:** Like leaves.
>
> **Vladimir:** Like sand.
>
> **Estragon:** Like leaves.
>
> *Silence.*
>
> **Vladimir:** They all speak at once.
>
> **Estragon:** Each one to itself.
>
> *Silence.*
>
> **Vladimir:** Rather they whisper
>
> **Estragon:** They rustle.
>
> **Vladimir:** They murmur.
>
> **Estragon:** They rustle.
>
> *Silence.*
>
> **Vladimir:** What do they say?

> Estragon: They talk about their lives.
>
> Vladimir: To have lived is not enough for them.
>
> Estragon: They have to talk about it.
>
> Vladimir: To be dead is not enough for them.
>
> Estragon: It is not sufficient.
>
> *Silence.*
>
> Vladimir: They make a noise like feathers.
>
> Estragon: Like leaves.
>
> Vladimir: Like ashes.
>
> Estragon: Like leaves.[25]

As I have written, my mother never converted to Judaism. It would have taken resolve to turn around something as primal as her Catholicism, which would not have been her way. She was a natural Zen master who knew how to take the path of least resistance. If it were not essential to our daily life, I'm sure she saw no good reason to do it. And she was right. She was not in any way a religious person (as far as I know), so it didn't seem to matter much to her that she was almost always among Jews, except when she or the two of us were with her family—the Polish Catholics—or with the Italians that surrounded us in Brooklyn and long ago had adopted us as part of their family. Nonetheless, in my mother's pocketbook there was always a perfumed handkerchief with embroidery along the edges and next to it, a rosary. Unlike my Aunt Helen, she did not go through the beads contemplatively each day. In fact, I never saw her use it, except for the few times when we were together at church in Pennsylvania. Perhaps she kept it close out of habit or just in case.

In the evening of the day that my mother died, after everyone had gone and Jack was asleep, I sat down to meditate. I cried, of course, choosing the same place on the floor where the noisy inflatable mattress had been for all those long, interminable nights. I felt calm just being close to her bed. Behind me was the low coffee table my parents had brought with them from Brooklyn. I noted that for the first time ever it was clear of all clutter. But at the moment that I turned around to get up, I noticed something on the table, which, some minutes before, had been completely empty. It was a saint's card, the kind you might buy in a church and carry in your bag for protection. And although I had been through her drawers many times, I had never seen this one before.

It was small, like a playing card, glossy, and deep Mediterranean blue, with miniature gold filigree beads weaving around the edges of the front to make a rosary that ended in a small cross. I suppose one could touch the little, raised dots one at a time, for contemplation. When I turned it over, there was a miniature photo of a porcelain statue of the Virgin and Child surrounded by a background of robin's egg blue—very delicate. I felt immediately that this was a card from my mother to me. It was a card to say, "I will always be your mother. You will always be my child." It stunned me to see it there, and I've kept it on my altar ever since.

This event also marked the beginning of a new relationship with my mother, one that would take place in actions noted on the physical plane that would somehow, inexplicably yet clearly, link us together on the astral plane. Things would be relocated, or they would disappear and reappear. There would be dreams with sparse language or a singular image, just enough to lift me out of sadness and assure me that we were still connected. In rare moments, my mother would show herself to me in dreams at various ages. At times there would be familiar humor, sarcasm, and wit connected to these interventions, to convince me that, indeed, it was her, finding a way to stay close to me.

When I was writing in Rome after her death, I immersed myself daily in Renaissance painting. I was struck then (and still am) by the way those artists created scenarios to portray communication between the spiritual and secular worlds, which, for them, were often literally just an arm's length away. How easy it seemed to achieve this communication visually; how hard it is to do in language. Everyone at that time accepted the organic relationship between these states of consciousness. Now, it is difficult to achieve this intimacy in any form without appearing to have "lost your marbles," as Rose might say.

The Accademia

∽

Gravity makes things come down, wings make them rise.[26]

Many years ago, when I first entered the Gallerie dell'Accademia in Venice, the great repository of Renaissance painting,

I was completely knocked over by the enormous sixteenth-century narrative paintings of Tintoretto, Tiepolo, Carpaccio, and others, in which angels and forces outside the landscape become essential to the earthly narrative taking place. I was fascinated with the iconography that allowed angels to jump into complex situations and intervene on behalf of those deserving mortals who needed assistance. I was astounded by how close the world of "God" seemed. Angels were often sitting on clouds, looking down at humans, as humans looked up to heaven, expectantly—as if these distinct levels of consciousness were in constant dialogue.

In Tintoretto's enormous *Miracle of the Slave*, my favorite of them all, a male figure lies naked on the ground in the center of a crowd that is pushing and shoving, almost trampling him to death. Their proximity and the architecture create an alarmingly claustrophobic scenario. One man is holding up the instruments—the bone-breaking and shattering tools that are about to be used to torture the slave. The slave's crime (we are told in the catalogue) is that he has "venerated the relics of a saint," defying his master's prohibition. Just as the brutality is about to take place, an upside-down angel (St. Mark) appears. With feet pointing straight up to heaven and a hand pointing to earth, the angel gestures to the slave, swooping down to save him and, of course, the other mortals from the sin of murdering a fellow human—the angel in position, about to perform a miracle.

Defying gravity, the angel's orange robe does not fly up, even though the angel is hovering at a 90-degree angle to the earth. But neither the angel nor the dress is subject to natural laws. When a human wearing a skirt is inverted, the skirt blows up, but not here. In dropping down to the "mundane plane," as Blake might call it, angels negotiate a very different set of laws.

What wings raised to the second power can make things come down without weight?[27]

After my mother died, the logic of gravity and the physical world often became similarly inverted. Things happened that could not be explained and that I did not want to explain.

God crosses through the thickness to come to us.[28]

I merely wanted to keep them in memory. They were my conversations with my mother and, as such, were private. But every now and then, one became public.

My mother died in November. On my first birthday after her death, April 6, I was in Milan for the Design Fair with a group of colleagues. We had brought an installation produced by students to the fair and, on the evening of April 5, we were holding a celebratory dinner to honor them. I was leaving the restaurant with my friends, Lisa and a young Italian architect named Antonio. In the madness of the fair, we could not get a cab back to the hotel in the center of Milan, so we decided to walk, and Antonio offered to accompany us. It was late, almost midnight, and we were enjoying the gorgeous night. At some point, Lisa started counting down. "It's almost your birthday," she said. "Approaching midnight. It's getting closer." As we walked I began to feel terribly sad. It was my first birthday since my mother died—my birthday but her day of giving birth to me. "Almost your birthday," Lisa laughed. And then she began: "Ten, nine, eight, seven, six, five, four, three, two, one. Happy birthday!" At that exact moment, a bouquet of three balloons, which we previously had not seen, floated down from the night sky and landed at our feet. I began to cry. Lisa began to cry. We stood in amazement. The balloons stayed for only a moment, and then suddenly they separated and the wind slowly took them away separately in the order they had arrived—one, two, three, and they were gone.

We stood under the lamppost and wept, Lisa perhaps more astonished than either Antonio or me. Its miraculous nature not unknown to me, I recognized the event immediately as a birthday gesture from my mother. Antonio just smiled. He's Italian and a student of Renaissance art; he knew a miracle when he saw one. But Lisa, who had no clear way to absorb what had just occurred, kept exclaiming—"Did you see that? Did you see that? It's your mother. It's a gift from your mother. I can feel it," she said, tears running down her cheeks. It was a "break in the ceiling,"[29] as Simone Weil might say. Lisa and I have talked and cried about it together on my birthdays almost every year since.

There have been other minor miracles over the years that followed, too many to describe here, too small to mention—

although, can any miracle really be too small? But this one and one other were witnessed by others, and, with certainty, existed outside my own imagination.

The Unveiling: The Return

~

Henceforth and forever I am my own mother.[30]

I have always loved the concept of the "unveiling" of the stone in Jewish law. It marks the year since a death—a moment of recognition that would be met with tears in any case—and occurs at the gravesite, with family and friends, as an end to the mourning, an end to the reciting of the *Kaddish*.

The day of my mother's unveiling, it rained and rained and rained—just like her funeral, just like her death. By the time we got to the cemetery, it had almost stopped. This time I had asked two close friends—Judy and Annie—and Jack, of course, to accompany me. We were to be met by Beulah and the rabbi.

The stone already was to have been set in place and covered with a cloth until the prayers were read. But weeks before the stone was to be cut, I had received a call from Beth El Cemetery asking for my mother's Hebrew name. I had not anticipated that my non-Jewish mother would also need a Hebrew name on her tombstone. I told them I'd call back, stalling. I had to find a name, fast. I went online to locate an appropriate one beginning with H, for Helen. There was a long list. I chose Hadara. It means *Bedecked by Beauty*. And so I named my mother the Beautiful One, because she always was.

Once again it seemed I was constructing her Jewishness. But, as Melville wrote to Hawthorne at the completion of *Moby Dick*, "I have written a wicked book and feel as spotless as a lamb."[31] I, too, felt no guilt. I was only completing my assignment, making sure she could be buried with my father as she had chosen, her stone in place for eternity beside his. She had paid her fees for her plot (now up to fifteen dollars a year). She was part of this family. She had a right. And now we, she and I, were very close to finishing the task.

All the stones in Beth El Cemetery are the same silver-gray, sparkly granite. And, at the Citron Circle, there was only one kind of stone marker allowed—flat to the ground, etched in the same typeface—because Jews believe that all are equal in death, and so it would be.

I agonized over what the stone should say. Because her friends were among her greatest assets—and her ability to keep making new ones after she'd outlived so many surely her true gift—I added "friend" to the epitaph. In this way those outside the "family" who also loved her would be acknowledged. In the end, they were the ones who stayed closest. They had not abandoned her when she became old, hard of hearing, and bound to her apartment. They continued to miss her, to remember her, to idealize her strength. Finally, too, it was her friendship with my Aunt Helen—her sister-in-law—that had given her such profound and loving companionship and allowed her to sustain her independence in the last years. Those "Two Helens," as they were known, were sisters of the soul.

And so the stone reads:

> Helen Hadara Becker
> 1909–2005
> Beloved Wife, Mother, and Friend

When my father died, I floated without anchor, a free fall into eternity. This was different. I now understood that the only way to keep her close was to keep death close. I would have dreaded this long ago, but now I feared more that she and the memory of our life together would be lost to me forever.

Once again, Jack and I had rented a car to travel back to New Jersey. Jack was driving. It was raining. This time, as we entered the cemetery, a large, dappled hawk appeared, flying very low in the sky. Now at eye level with my passenger window and just inches from me, the bird stayed in close formation, hugging the passenger side of the car from the cemetery gates to the burial site. When we arrived at the obelisk, the bird flew up to a branch and looked out over the entire Citron Circle and all of us.

The ceremony began. The rabbi read the Twenty-Third Psalm in Hebrew and in English—the Psalm of Mercy—and then the *Kaddish*, the words I had recited all my life in memory of those I had loved: "*Yit-ga-dal v'yit-ka-dash sh'mei ra-ba /*

b'al-ma-di-v'ra-khir'ute. . . ." And then the prayer: "Grant true rest upon the wings of the *Shechinah*—the Divine Presence." After all this, the official acts of mourning were complete. I had done what she had asked. I had "put the ashes to rest." We had put the ashes to rest.

I watched the hawk, and it watched me. The prayers over, the bird took flight.

Beulah clutched my hand in her felt glove, and I clutched back. All was gray now, the ubiquitous rain an imperceptible mist.

NOTES

1. Simone Weil, *Gravity and Grace*, trans. Arthur Willis (Lincoln, NE: University of Nebraska Press, 1952), 69.
2. Ibid., 48.
3. Elizabeth U. Harding, *Kali: The Black Goddess of Dakshineswar* (York Beach, ME: Nicholas-Hays, 1993), 164–65.
4. Hannah Kliger, *Jewish Hometown Association and Family Circles in New York: The WPA Yiddish Writers' Group Study* (New York: Municipal Archives, 1992).
5. Harding, *Kali*, 102.
6. Weil, *Gravity and Grace*, 68.
7. Sandra Edelman, *Turning the Gorgon: A Meditation on Shame* (Putnam, CT: Spring Publications, 1998), 33.
8. Ibid., 77.
9. Ibid., 33.
10. Harding, *Kali*, 43.
11. Sushila Blackman, *Graceful Exits: How Great Beings Die, Death Stories of Hindu, Tibetan, Buddhist, and Zen Masters* (Boston: Shambhala, 1997).
12. Weil, *Gravity and Grace*, 199.
13. Ibid., 56.
14. Ibid., 180.
15. Ibid., 170.
16. John Milton, *Paradise Lost*, ed. Gordon Teskey (New York: Norton, 2005), 282.
17. Weil, *Gravity and Grace*, 68.

18. Theodore Roethke, "The Far Field," in *The Collected Poems of Theodore Roethke* (New York: Anchor Books, 1975), 194.

19. The Heart Sutra

20. Weil, *Gravity and Grace*, 174.

21. Ibid., 127.

22. Roethke, *Collected Poems*, 87.

23. Harding, *Kali*, 31.

24. Weil, *Gravity and Grace*, 45.

25. Samuel Beckett, *Waiting for Godot: A Tragicomedy in Two Acts* (New York: Grove Press, 1954), 69.

26. Weil, *Gravity and Grace*, 48.

27. Ibid.

28. Ibid., 142.

29. Ibid., 149.

30. Roland Barthes, *Mourning Diary*, trans. Richard Howard (New York: Hill and Wang, 2009), 36.

31. Herman Melville, *The Letters of Herman Melville,* eds Merrell R. Davis and William H. Gilman (New Haven: Yale University Press, 1960), 77.

BIOGRAPHICAL NOTE

Carol Becker has written several books and numerous essays for print and online publications on various topics, including the intellectual lives and emotional well-being of women. Her recently reissued book, *The Invisible Drama: Women and the Anxiety of Change*, has been translated into six languages and is available worldwide. Her other areas of focus include art and social responsibility, education, and the emerging trends in global culture.

Becker is Professor of the Arts and Dean of Faculty at Columbia University School of the Arts in the City of New York.

She is a former professor of literature and philosophy at the School of the Art Institute of Chicago, where she was also Dean of Faculty. Becker has received numerous prestigious awards for her work as a writer and an influential leader in the education of artists. As a prominent voice writing on feminist issues and the contemporary art world, she is also the frequent subject of articles and interviews.

DISCARD

CPSIA information can be obtained at www.ICGtesting.com
Printed in the USA
BVOW02s0853030916

460929BV00002B/10/P